THE TURBULENT
LONDON OF RICHARD II

THE TURBULENT
LONDON OF RICHARD II

BY

RUTH BIRD, M.A. (Lond.)

WITH AN INTRODUCTION BY
THE LATE
JAMES TAIT, M.A., Litt.D., F.B.A.
FORMERLY PROFESSOR OF ANCIENT AND MEDIAEVAL HISTORY
IN THE UNIVERSITY OF MANCHESTER

WITH A MAP OF FOURTEENTH CENTURY LONDON
BY
MARJORIE B. HONEYBOURNE, M.A. (Lond.)

LONGMANS, GREEN AND CO
LONDON ◆ NEW YORK ◆ TORONTO

LONGMANS, GREEN AND CO LTD
6 & 7 CLIFFORD STREET LONDON W I
ALSO AT MELBOURNE AND CAPE TOWN

LONGMANS, GREEN AND CO INC
55 FIFTH AVENUE NEW YORK 3

LONGMANS, GREEN AND CO
215 VICTORIA STREET TORONTO I

ORIENT LONGMANS LTD
BOMBAY CALCUTTA MADRAS

First published   1949

PRINTED IN GREAT BRITAIN AT
THE UNIVERSITY PRESS
ABERDEEN

PREFACE

THE unavoidable delay in the publication of this monograph, caused by the war, has robbed me of the opportunity of publicly thanking the late Dr. James Tait for his great kindness in writing the introduction, the late Miss E. Jeffries Davis, M.A., for constantly and generously placing at my disposal her unique knowledge of the history of London, or the late J. W. Allen, M.A., to whom I owe any power I may possess of dealing with a historical problem. I can only put on record my gratitude to them all.

My acknowledgments and thanks are also due to Dr. A. H. Thomas, for his unfailing help and his patience with my questions when he was Deputy Keeper of the Records to the Corporation of London ; to Dr. V. H. Galbraith for his advice ; to Miss M. B. Honeybourne, M.A., for allowing me to use her valuable map ; to the Corporation of the City of London for permission to publish the letter to Lord Zouch ; to the Worshipful Company of Goldsmiths for permission to examine and use their manuscript records ; to Bedford College for Women, both for awarding me the Amy Lady Tate Scholarship from 1921-22 when the first draft of this monograph was made, as a London M.A. Thesis, and for making a grant towards its publication in a revised form ; to the University of London also for a grant towards publication ; and to the Governors of the Wyggeston Grammar School for Girls, Leicester, for a year's leave of absence, during 1935-36, in the latter part of which I was able to revise and rewrite my first study.

RUTH BIRD.

January, 1948.

CONTENTS

vii

LIST OF ABBREVIATIONS USED IN THE FOOTNOTES

CORRIGENDA

Page 39, line 19, *for* Council *read* Councils.
Page 46, last word of footnote 4, *for* John *read* Adam.

BIBLIOGRAPHY

PRIMARY SOURCES

Manuscript

A.—PUBLIC RECORD OFFICE.

I. RECORDS OF THE DUCHY OF LANCASTER.

(a) Miscellaneous Books : *Registers of Grants, Charters, Leases, etc.* No. 14. *Register of John, Duke of Lancaster, Temp. Richard II.* (This is a register of grants, appointments, warrants for the paying out of money, and other similar transactions, authorised by the Duke's Privy Seal, for the period January 1379–80—July 1383.)

(b) Accounts Various, Bundle III, No. 1. (Receiver-General of John, Duke of Lancaster, 1376–77.)

Accounts Various, Bundle III, No. 2. (Receiver-General of John, Duke of Lancaster, 1392–93.)

Accounts Various, Bundle XXXII, No. 21. (Certificates of the accounts of the Receiver-General of John, Duke of Lancaster and Guienne, 1393–94.)

(Given as (?2–3 Ric. II) Lists and Indexes No. XIV, p. 20 ; this error is corrected in the copy in the Literary Search Room in the P.R.O.)

Accounts Various, Bundle I, No. 1. (Household Accounts of Henry, Earl of Derby, 1381–82.)

Accounts Various, Bundle I, No. 2. (Household Accounts of Henry, Earl of Derby, 1387–88.)

Accounts Various, Bundle I, No. 3. (Wardrobe Accounts of Henry, Earl of Derby, 1390–91.)

(c) Manuscript Calendars in the Record Office of Ancient Deeds Press 27, Nos. 83A and 84.

II. ANCIENT PETITIONS.

(a) Nos. 1000–1005 (inclusive) : the petitions of the Embroiderers, Leathersellers, Founders, Pinners, Painters and Armourers against Brembre and Exton (1386).

(b) No. 6417 : the petition of John de Northampton against his sentence. Transcribed in Appendix VI.

III. CORAM REGE ROLLS.

(a) No. 507 : the inquisitions taken at the trial of John de Northampton—partly printed by Powell and Trevelyan : *The Peasants' Rising and the Lollards,* pp. 27–38, partly transcribed in Appendix IV.

(*b*) No. 488 : inquisitions taken concerning Londoners suspected of rebellion in 1381 : The Transcript in *Le Soulèvement des Travailleurs d'Angleterre* (Réville) omit the names of the jurors, among other less important details.

IV. PATENT ROLL. I, Richard II, Part I, membrane 12.

V. RETURNS TO WRITS, No. 9 : the return made by Southwark to the summons to the Parliament of February 1387–88.

VI. MS. CALENDAR INQUISITIONES POST MORTEM.

B.—RECORDS OF THE CITY OF LONDON. Preserved in the Guildhall.

(*a*) PLEA AND MEMORANDA ROLLS.
These Rolls take the place of the Mayor's Court Rolls for the period 1324–1484. They have been calendared in full to 1381 and a select number of them from 1381–1412, by Dr. A. H. Thomas.

(*b*) HUSTINGS ROLLS.
These rolls contain all deeds and wills enrolled in the Hustings Court between 1252 and 1717. The wills have been calendared by Dr. Sharpe, but not always with complete accuracy ; to the deeds there is a manuscript index under the names of the principal parties to each conveyance. This, again, has occasional slips.

(*c*) FILES OF MAYORS' COURT ROLLS for the reigns of Edward III and Richard II.

(*d*) LETTER BOOK H.
Note.—There are no fourteenth-century records of the Sheriffs' Court—i.e. the court in which debtors were sued—except for the years 1318–21.

(*e*) GUILDHALL LIBRARY ORIGINAL DEEDS, MS. 36.

C.—RECORDS OF THE LIVERY COMPANIES OF LONDON.
Goldsmiths' Wardens' Accounts and Court Minutes.
Book A, Part I, 1332–1442.
Book A, Part II, 1372–1446.
These are the earliest wardens' accounts.

D.—SOMERSET HOUSE WILLS.
Episcopal Registers.
Commissary of London (Courtney).
Commissary of London (Broun).
Commissary of London (Prowet).
Prerogative Court of Canterbury.

Printed

I. CHRONICLES.

(*a*) *The Anominalle Chronicle*, ed. V. H. Galbraith—of particular value for the "Good" Parliament and the Peasants' Revolt.

(*b*) *Chronicon Angliae* (Rolls Series).

(*c*) Walsingham : *Historia Anglicana*, 2 vols. (Rolls Series).

(*d*) *Chronicon Adae de Usk* (ed. E. Maunde Thompson).

(*e*) Continuation of *Adam of Murimuth*—1384 (Rolls Series).

(*f*) *Chronique de la Traïson*, ed. Williams.

(*g*) *Eulogium Historiarum*, Vol. III (Rolls Series).

(*h*) *Chronicle of Thomas Favent* (Bod. Misc. MSS. 2963), ed. M. McKisack (Camden Miscellany Vol. XIV)—probably by an eye-witness of the Merciless Parliament.

(*i*) Higden : Vol. IX (Rolls Series). The continuation of the Polychronicon from 1381–94 printed in this volume was claimed in 1907 by Dean Armitage Robinson as the work of a Westminster monk (" an unrecognised Westminster Chronicler "). In addition to the proofs brought forward in this paper, attention may be called to the long and accurate extracts which this chronicler gives from the Parliament Rolls. Very full details are given also in London matters.

(*j*) *Historia Vitae et Regni Ricardi Secundi* (ed. Hearne).

(*k*) Knighton, Vol. II (Rolls Series).

(*l*) *Otterbourne* (ed. Hearne).

(*m*) *Chronicles of London* (ed. Kingsford). The first chronicle in this volume (Julius BII) is alone of contemporary value, and only for 1399.

II. MISCELLANEOUS.

(*a*) *Ricardi Maydiston de Concordia inter Regem Ricardum II et Civitatem Londonie* (Camden Society).

(*b*) *Excerpta Historica*, ed. Sam. Bentley. Transcript of the Will of William Walworth.

(*c*) Williams, E. *Early Holborn*. (P.C.C.).

(*d*) " The Confession of Thomas Usk " (printed in *London English*, ed. Chambers and Daunt).

(*e*) *Records of the Borough of Northampton*, 2 vols. 1898.

III. PUBLIC RECORDS.

(*a*) *Accompts of the Manor of the Savoy*, ed. Walton.

(*b*) Calendar of Charter Rolls, 1341–1417.

(*c*) Calendar of Close Rolls, 1369–99.

(*d*) Calendar of Fine Rolls, 1377–99.

(*e*) Calendar of Patent Rolls, 1369–1422.

(*f*) *Diplomatic Correspondence of Richard II*, ed. Ed. Perroy (Royal Hist. Soc.).

(*g*) Lists and Indexes, XLIX (Diplomatic Documents).

(*h*) Extracts from the Issue Rolls, Henry III—Henry IV, ed. Devon.

(i) Issue Rolls of Thomas de Brantingham (ed. Devon).

(j) John of Gaunt's Register, 1372–76, ed. S. Armitage Smith (Camden Society).

(k) London and Middlesex Feet of Fines, Vol I, ed. W. J. Hardy and W. Page, 1892.

(l) Official Returns of Members of Parliament, Vol. I.

(m) Reports of Deputy Keeper of Duchy of Lancaster Records.

    (1) No. 32. Appendix I (4), Calendar of Chancery Rolls, 1377–89.

    (2) No. 40. Appendix I (4), Calendar of Patent Rolls, 1381–87.

    (3) No. 43. Appendix I (3), Calendar of Privy Seals Richard II.

    (4) No. 35. Appendix I (1), Calendar of Ancient Charters or Grants.

    (5) No. 36. Appendix I (2), Calendar of Ancient Charters or Grants continued.

(n) Rolls of Parliament, Vols. 2 and 3.

(o) Select Cases in Chancery (Selden Society).

(p) Select Cases in the Exchequer Chamber before all the Justices of England, 1377–1461.

(q) Select Cases before the King's Council (Selden Society).

(r) Statutes of the Realm, Vols. I and II.

IV. CITY OF LONDON RECORDS.

(a) Calendars of Letter Books A–L inclusive (ed. R. R. Sharpe).

(b) Calendar of Wills proved in the Court of Husting, 2 vols. (ed. R. R. Sharpe).

(c) *Historical Charters of the City of London* (ed. W. D. Birch).

(d) *Liber Albus* (ed. Riley).

(e) *Liber Custumarum* (ed. Riley).

(f) *Memorials* (ed. Riley).

(g) Calendar of Early Mayors' Court Rolls, 1298–1307, ed. A. H. Thomas.

(h) Calendars of Plea and Memoranda Rolls, 1324–64, 1364–81, 1381–1412, ed. A. H. Thomas.

V. RECORDS OF THE LIVERY COMPANIES.

Note.—Various works containing extracts only from records otherwise irrelevant to the subject will be found in the list of secondary authorities.

(a) Petitions of the Drapers against Brembre (Ancient petitions No. 4664), printed by A. H. Johnson in his *History of the Worshipful Company of Drapers*, Vol. I, pp. 208–11.

(b) Ancient Records of the Merchant Taylors, printed by C. M. Clode in *Memorials of the Merchant Taylors' Company*.

(c) Facsimile of MS. archives of the Company of Grocers (ed. J. A. Kingdon).

Note.—There are no records extant for 1375–78, 1380–82, 1384, 1388–96.

The editor thinks this is due to deliberate action on the part of contemporaries, and cites Adam Bamme's proclamation when mayor which forbids Northampton or Brembre to be spoken of. This contention is weakened by the presence of records for the critical years 1383, 1387, 1388—and cf. J. Watney in *The Mercers' Company*: "There is a gap in the company's records for 1348–91. All their proceedings were fully entered in an old red book of the Mercery, which might be seen of any of the fraternity on occasion, but it was voted that to copy them in the fair book of Wardens' Accounts was more trouble than profit. But ' le viele papier rouge ' has long disappeared."

(d) Documents concerning Vintners' Hall in Millbourne's *Vintners' Company*.

(e) Records of the Saddlers in J. W. Sherwell's *History of the Saddlers' Company*.

(f) Records of the Cutlers in C. Welch's *History of the Cutlers' Company*.

B.—SECONDARY AUTHORITIES.

I. EARLY CHRONICLES. Fifteenth and sixteenth centuries.

(a) The Brut (ed. Brie).

(b) Chronicle of the Grey Friars of London (ed. Nichols) (Camden Society).

(c) Chronicles of London (ed. Kingsford). The first chronicle in this volume (I Julius B. II) is of contemporary value for 1399. See list of primary sources.

(d) An English Chronicle of the Reign of Richard II, Henry IV, Henry V and Henry VI (ed. Davies) (Camden Society), (written before 1471).

(e) Fabyan: New Chronicles of England and France, 1516 edn. ed. Ellis, 1811.

(f) Grafton's Chronicle.

(g) Gregory's Chronicle (ed. Gairdner), in *Collection of a London Citizen* (Camden Society).

(h) Harleian 565 (ed. Nicolas). Probably written in the reign of Henry IV.

(i) Lambeth MS. 306: Three Fifteenth-Century Chronicles (ed. Gairdner) (Camden Society).

II. MISCELLANEOUS WORKS.

Ravenhill, W.: *The Case of the Company of Grocers*, 1686. Stow *Survey of London* (ed. Kingsford).

III. MODERN WORKS.

Armitage-Smith, S.: *John of Gaunt*.
Baddeley, J. J.: *The Aldermen of Cripplegate Ward*.
Bagshaw, S.: *Kent*. Vol. I.

Baldwin, S. E.: "Records of the Duchy of Lancaster" (*Bulletin of the Institute of Historical Research IV*).

Beaven, A. B.: *The Aldermen of London*. 2 vols.

Carus-Wilson, E. M.: "The Merchant Adventurers" (*Economic History Review*, Vol. IV.).

Clarke, M. V.: *Fourteenth Century Studies*.

Clode, C. M.: *Memorials of the Merchant Taylors*.

Clode, C. M.: *Early History of the Merchant Taylors*. 2 vols.

Consitt, F.: *The London Weavers' Company*. Vol. I.

Cunningham, W.: *The Growth of English Industry and Commerce*. Vol. I.

Fisher, F.: *The Worshipful Company of Horners*.

Gross, C.: *The Gild Merchant*.

Gross, C.: *Sources and Literature of English History*.

Hasted's *History of Kent*.

Heath, J. B.: *Some Account of the Worshipful Company of Grocers of the City of London*.

Howell's *State Trials*. Vol. I.

Johnson, A. H.: *History of the Worshipful Company of Drapers*.

Kirk, R. E. G.: *Life Records of Chaucer*.

Lipson, E.: *An Introduction to the Economic History of England*. Vol. I.

ed. Little and Powicke: *Essays in Mediaeval History presented to T. F. Tout*.

Macaulay, J. S. A.: "The History of the Staple at Westminster in the reign of Richard II" (unprinted Oxford Thesis).

McKesack, M.: *Representation of English Boroughs in the Middle Ages*.

Mead, G. W. de C.: "The Financial Relations between the Crown and the City of London, Edward I to Henry VII (unprinted London Thesis).

Meyer, E. F.: (*Speculum VII*).

Nichols, J. G.: "The Vintners' Company" (*Transacts. Lond. and Middx. Archaeolog. Soc.* Vol. III).

Norton, G.: *The City of London*.

Oman, C.: *The Great Revolt of 1381*.

Page, W.: *London, its Origin and Early Development*.

Petit-Dutaillis, C.: *Studies Supplementary to Stubbs*. Vol. II.

Postan, M. and Power, E.: *English Trade in the 15th Century*.

Postan, M. M.: "Credit in Mediaeval Trade" (*Economic History Review*, 1928, pp. 234–61).

Powell and Trevelyan: *The Peasants' Rising and the Lollards*.

Prideaux, W. S.: *Memorials of the Goldsmiths' Company*.

Pulling, A. H.: *Laws and Customs of the City*.

Rees, J. A.: *The Worshipful Company of Grocers* (an Historical Retrospect).

Réville, A.: *Le Soulèvement des Travailleurs d'Angleterre en 1381*.

Rich, E. E.: "Mayors of the Staple" (*Cambridge Historical Journal*. Vol. IV, pp. 120–42).

Richardson, H. G.: "Heresy and The Lay Power under Richard II" (*English Historical Review* 1936, pp. 1–28.)

Robinson, J. A.: "An Unrecognised Westminster Chronicler" (*Proceedings of the British Academy* 1907, III, 61–77).

Rosedale, H. G.: *A Short History of the Worshipful Company of Horners.*

Sharpe, M.: "Records of the Duchy of Lancaster" (*Bulletin of Institute of Historical Research* XIII).

Sharpe, R. R.: *London and the Kingdom.* Vol. I.

Simon, A. L.: *History of the Wine Trade in England.* Vol. I.

Steel, A.: "English Government and Finance, 1377–1413" (*English Historical Review* 1936, pp. 29–51 and pp. 77–97).

Steel, A.: *Richard II.*

Stubbs, W.: *Constitutional History of England.* Vols. 2 and 3 (1883).

Tait, J.: *The Mediaeval English Borough.*

Thrupp, S.: "A Study of the Merchant Class of London in the 15th Century, with special reference to the Company of Grocers" (unprinted London Thesis).

Tout, T. F.: *Collected Papers.*

Tout, T. F.: *Chapters in Mediaeval Administrative History.*

Trevelyan, G.: *England in the Age of Wycliffe.*

Unwin, G.: *Finance and Trade under Edward III.*

Unwin, G.: *Gilds and Companies of London.*

Victoria County History of London.

Wadmore, J. F.: *History of the Skinners' Company.*

Watney, J.: *History of the Mercers' Company.*

American Historical Review. Vol. VII.

Bulletin of Institute of Historical Research. Vol. VII.

London Topographical Record. Vols. XI and XIV.

Transactions of the Royal Historical Society (4th Series). Vol. IV.

Dictionary of National Biography
  Articles on: Nicholas Brembre, John de Northampton, John Philpot, Michael de la Pole, Nicholas Twyford, John Waltham, William Walworth, Richard Whittington.

INTRODUCTION

In this book Miss Bird has made a solid contribution
to the elucidation of perhaps the most difficult episode in
the history of London and its relations to political parties.
I am glad that I have been asked to write an introduction,
because this gives me an opportunity of saying how much
I am impressed by the skill with which she has disentangled
the twisted threads of a most complicated series of events
and thrown new light upon much that had been still dark
to us.

The "Good" Parliament of 1376 ushered in a period of
revolution both in the City and in the State, and owing
to the proximity of London and Westminster the two
conflicts were constantly impinging on each other. This
interaction has tended to increase the obscurities caused
by the many cross-currents of civic faction. The results of
the two conflicts were different, for while the political
struggle ended in a change of dynasty, the municipal strife
was closed by the restoration of the *status quo* somewhat
modified.

Miss Bird, besides having at her disposal important
material which has only recently become easily accessible,
has subjected both the new and the old to a more detailed
examination than has been hitherto applied and has been
rewarded by some interesting results. When so many
different interests and motives were at work, the tendency
has been to concentrate on the more obvious and striking
and the problems have been too much simplified. Thus
the conflict between the victualling and the non-victualling
misteries became so much the centre of the civic strife as
to obscure the fact that it was only an economic cross-current,
though a violent one, in the secular clash between the
oligarchic court of aldermen and the commonalty. It did
not in fact originate in the City but in parliamentary
attempts under Edward III to cheapen food at the expense
of the trading exclusiveness of the boroughs generally.

Nor was it a question on which the aldermen presented a united front. They were wholesale merchants, capitalists, not as a body much interested in retail trade, except the fishmongers who were ranked as one of the most powerful of the great misteries at this date. Where they were all agreed was on the necessity of keeping the commonalty, which by this time had come to mean the lesser misteries or crafts, in due subordination, but the economic question was to introduce division in their ranks.

It was, however, no inkling of John of Northampton's plans for cheapening fish and humbling the fishmongers' mistery that compelled the aldermen in 1376 to submit to the revival of the stringent limitation of their re-election which had been the chief gain of the commonalty's short-lived victory in 1319 and to the substitution of the mistery for the ward with its alderman head as the electoral unit for the body, henceforth regularly known as the Common Council, in which they shared in the City government. Surrender was forced upon them by the general disgust at the " slander " which some of their number who made loans to the king and held financial commissions for him had brought upon the City by their corrupt dealings and at the critical moment by royal intervention.

That the new constitution survived the reactionary measures of John of Gaunt, though he secured the substitution of Nicholas Brembre for a mayor who had shown himself too sympathetic to the aims of its authors, is to be attributed more to the general resentment at the duke's attempt to extend the jurisdiction of the Earl Marshal over the City than to such elements of compromise as it seems to contain. His breach with the capitalist governing body was, however, of no good augury for the time when the opposition should have a more resolute mayor than Stable, and John's hostility should have been heightened by the contrast of his inefficiency on the renewal of war with France on Richard's accession with the active support in money and ships given by the City magnates.

It soon became evident that unless the opposition cap-tured the mayoralty and secured a sufficient footing in the body of aldermen, the reorganised Common Council was not to be depended on. The evidence collected by Miss Bird shows that the change of electoral unit made little difference in practice. The representatives of the lesser gilds were apparently no more apt to assert themselves against the bench of mayor and aldermen than were those of wards before or after.

Although the capitalist government showed want of resoluteness in the first stage of the Peasants' Revolt, neither party seems to have been involved, and a very belated attempt to convict some of the aldermen of treacherously admitting the insurgents into the city was, except in one case, clearly based on unconvincing evidence. There is some likelihood, indeed, that a truce in party strife in face of the common danger from the peasants and the lowest elements in the City may in part at least explain the absence of opposition to Northampton's election as mayor in October 1381. Not that he had up to this point done anything to alarm seriously any section of his opponents, and if he had confined himself to his campaign against the fishmongers' party feeling need not have been greatly stirred up. The prospect of cheap fish appealed to the poorer workers irrespective of politics, and the other great misteries had long been jealous of the special privileges which the fishmongers had secured from the Crown. Northampton thus obtained the support among the aldermen which was necessary if any policy was to be carried through. On a petition from the City a statute reaffirmed for cities and boroughs in general and for London in particular free trade in fresh fish and even excluded victuallers from judicial office. Nevertheless Northampton's party, though his followers belonged almost exclusively to the non-victualling misteries, cannot strictly be described as the non-victuallers' party since it did not include all the non-victuallers. It is not more exact to call it the party of the smaller misteries against the greater for members of all the great non-victualling misteries were found in its ranks.

The situation became more normal when Northampton began to turn his reforming campaign against the other great misteries from which the aldermen were drawn. It

was now a straight fight between the lesser and the greater
misteries, in other words between the commonalty and
the court of aldermen, as of old. In thus reuniting the
governing body against the new FitzOsbert or Hervey,
Northampton made a fatal mistake. With the king's
support a third mayoralty was averted and Brembre became
mayor. An attempt to whip up a popular movement made
Northampton's arrest and trial inevitable. John of Gaunt's
first open intervention on his behalf merely secured some
alleviation of the terms of his banishment from the City.
The constitutional changes of 1376, except annual election
of the aldermen, were repealed as was Northampton's
legislation against the fishmongers.

The City capitalists, who had made no loans to the Crown
during Northampton's tenure of office, now reopened their
purses to the king, and Brembre involved himself and the
City deeply with Richard in his conflict with the Lords
Appellant. Under his more cautious successor, Exton,
however, the aldermen yielded to superior force and opened
the gates to the Appellants, leaving Brembre to his fate in
the Merciless Parliament, but saving the City from sack
and their party from the return of Northampton and
reversal of the constitutional counter-revolution of 1384.
Free trade in fish was restored, but in the earlier Edwardian
form, not in Northampton's.

Richard, who had a long memory for injuries, never
forgot nor forgave this desertion. As soon as he recovered
power in 1389, he compelled the mayor and aldermen to
assent to the recall of Northampton, and two years later
at the petition of the Commons in Parliament he was
declared guiltless of the charges on which he had been
condemned and full restitution was ordered. This must have
disquieted the ruling party in the City, but they can hardly
have been prepared for the thunderbolt which Richard
launched in the following year. On the thinnest of pretexts,
the mayor, sheriffs and aldermen were put under arrest,
the liberties of the City were taken into the king's hand
and a royal warden was placed over it. Whether Richard
was unaware that this was illegal by a statute of 1354,
which required two previous offences, punished by fine,

before this grave action could be taken, or whether in the first heat of his revenge he ignored it, cannot be decided, but whichever was the case, a belated and clumsy attempt was made to conform to the statute by charging the officers of two years before with the requisite two " defects of good government " and inflicting the statutory fines! Having sufficiently vented his rancour, Richard, at the supplications of the queen and the citizens, pardoned the delinquents, forgave their fines—though the City had to pay £10,000—and removed his warden.

This outrageous exhibition of deferred spite and misuse of legal forms might well have roused fears among the Lords Appellant that their turn might come next, but there is no evidence that they saw the writing on the wall.

It was now the rulers of the City who had a smarting injury to resent secretly until the day came when it could be avenged. When there were added the " blank charters " and other extortions of Richard's last two years, it is not surprising that the revolution of 1399 was welcomed by the City.

Meanwhile, the aldermen had been quietly repairing the last of the breaches in their power which had been made in 1376. Two years after the wardenship they finally got rid of their annual election and became irremovable. Vacancies were filled by the mayor and aldermen from two (four from 1402) nominated by the ward. Northampton had had no influence after his return and died in 1397.

By 1400 London had a firmly-established mercantile oligarchy which had only to realise that financial support was as essential to the central government in peace as in war to play an important part in national politics. Oligarchic though its administration was, it escaped the worst features of that closing of the borough corporations which was far advanced by the end of the Middle Ages, an escape which it owed in no small measure to the crises through which it passed in the last quarter of the fourteenth century. The clause of the Statute of 1341 which empowered the mayor and aldermen to provide a remedy for customs which proved defective, but only with the assent of the commonalty, never became a mere dead letter. The new Common Council of 1376, freed of its gild organisation and firmly based on the primitive local divisions of the City, had features which brought it safely through the revolutionary stage to express the voice of the citizens at large in civic legislation and in the choice of City officers. The canker of co-option did not find entrance into the governing bodies of the City and so, with needful adjustments to later conditions from time to time, they alone survived the Reform Act of 1835 and still transact the business of an otherwise transformed community.

JAMES TAIT.

CHAPTER I

THE LONDONERS AND THEIR LEADERS
IN 1376

In the London of 1376 at least four classes can be distinguished—apart altogether from the clergy, and from those servants of lords with houses in the City, who were, for that reason, sometimes temporary, sometimes permanent, inhabitants of London. There is first a small group of wealthy merchant capitalists who were closely connected with one another and with foreign merchants, and, in most cases, with the Crown also. They belonged in the main to five misteries—the vintners, fishmongers, grocers, mercers and goldsmiths, though one very prominent capitalist of 1376, Adam de Bury, was a skinner. They dominated the government of the City by a virtual monopoly of the offices of mayor and alderman; but this monopoly was about to be questioned by two other classes of Londoners—the small masters of various crafts, and an intermediate group of men whose trade was wide enough, and property large enough, to make them the natural leaders of the small master class within their misteries, and to give them less narrow interests than those of that class. Such men are to be found amongst the aldermen of 1376, but are only in the minority; their position and power were altogether insignificant in comparison with those of the great capitalists.

The fourth important class was that of the unenfranchised, the non-citizen; this included not only the apprentices and journeymen, some of whom, though probably not the majority, would eventually become citizens in the full sense of the term, but also the casual labourers, " a mass of destitution, misfortune and rascality," according to Dr. A. H. Thomas; [1] their importance in the City lay in their

[1] *Intro. Cal. Plea and Mem. Rolls*, 1364–81, p. lxiv.

numbers, and in the threat to life and property which came from them in those moments of crisis and conflict which occur so frequently in London in the last quarter of the fourteenth century.

The two men whose personal rivalry is so closely inter-mingled with so much of this conflict, Nicholas Brembre and John de Northampton, illustrate very plainly the differences between a member of the capitalist class and a leader of the small masters.

There is mention of only one Brembre in the City Records, apart from the famous mayor of that name; he is a certain clerk, Sir Thomas de Brembre, to whom there are two unimportant references, in 1349[1] and 1353.[2] But if Nicholas Brembre, like so many London citizens,[3] did not found his fortunes on an already established family connection with the City, he was by his marriage closely connected with a very important group of men there. His wife was Idonia, one, and probably the eldest,[4] of the four daughters and co-heiresses of John de Stodeye, vintner, who died in 1376. They had then been married for at least seven years.[5]

Stodeye was a man of great wealth,[6] he gave financial assistance on several occasions to Edward III's government and held various official positions under it. Of Brembre's two married sisters-in-law, one was first the wife of John Birlyngham,[7] mercer, and, on his death, of John Philipot or Philpot, grocer;[8] the other was married to Henry Vanner, vintner.[9] Birlyngham and Vanner were wealthy,

---

[1] Cal. Plea and Mem. Rolls, 1323–64, p. 230.

[2] H.R. 81. 15. Hasted speaks of Nicholas Brembre as the son of Sir John Brembre; Hist. of Kent, II, p. 258, but gives no reference.

[3] See Thomas, Introd. Cal. P. and M.R. pp. xxxii–xxxiv.

[4] When the four sisters are mentioned together her name always comes first and in the will disposing of his personal property (Commiss. of Lond. Regist. Books, Courtenay, fos. 39 and 40) her then unmarried sister, Johanna, was left in her guardianship and that of her husband.

[5] H.R. 97. 152 dors.

[6] See George Unwin, Finance and Trade under Edward III, pp. 296–7.

[7] Commiss. of Lond. Regist. Books, Courtenay, fos. 39 and 40.

[8] By October 1376, Cal. L.B.H, p. 49.

[9] Commiss. of Lond. Regist. Books, Courtenay, fos. 39 and 40. For the connections and descendants of John de Stodeye, see Appendix I.

and of standing in the City, but Philpot was already in the closing years of Edward III far more than this, and under Richard II was to achieve an influence and fame which in some ways exceeded those of his better known contemporary William Walworth; they were certainly approached by those of no other merchant of the early years of that reign.

From Stodeye, Idonia and Nicholas Brembre inherited valuable gold and silver plate, as well as a fourth part of nearly all his extensive real property, much of which was in the City itself.[1] Before the death of his father-in-law, however, Brembre was already the possessor of a great deal of real property. In 1373 he owned the " hospicium " in La Ryole in the Vintry [2] where we know he was living in 1381 [3] and between 1369, in which year there occurs the first entry concerning him in the Hustings Rolls,[4] and 1376, he acquired lands, tenements and rents in the parishes of St. Peter Cornhill,[4] St. Stephen Coleman Street,[5] St. Martin Vintry,[6] St. Olave Old Jewry and All Hallows Staining Church,[7] St. Margaret Lothbury,[8] St. Michael Paternoster,[9] St. James Garlickhithe [10] and St. Nicholas Acon.[11] Outside London he held land both in Middlesex [12] and Kent.[13] Together with Walworth, Philipot and John Aubrey, grocer, he held lands and tenements in the parishes of St. Mary Woolchurch, St. Michael Cornhill and St. Christopher.[14] After Stodeye's death he gained still more property in St. Olave Old Jewry [15] and St. Michael

---

[1] One tenement is left to a nephew, but the rest divided between his four daughters. There are legacies in money for the repair of London Bridge and a bridge in Holborn, and for other religious and charitable purposes, and one of £200 to his unmarried daughter which might have had to have been met by at least a partial sale of his real property (Brembre, Philpot and Vanner were among his executors), *Commiss. of Lond. Regist. Books, Courtenay*, fos. 39 and 40.

[2] *H.R.* 101. 117.   [3] *Réville*, p. 207.   [4] *H.R.* 97. 152 dors.

[5] *Ibid.* 98. 77.   [6] *Ibid.* 98. 132.   [7] *Ibid.* 98. 48.

[8] *Ibid.* 101. 45 and Sharpe: *Cal. of Wills*, II, p. 144.

[9] *H.R.* 101. 152. Houses in addition to that where he lived which was also in this parish.   [10] *Ibid.* 103. 57.   [11] *Ibid.* 103. 205.

[12] *Ibid.* 99. 9 and 99. 19; *Cal. P.R.*, 12 December 1371, m. 7.

[13] *Ibid.* 16 March 1373, m. 21.

[14] *Ibid.* 104. 5. Two other entries which concern Brembre, 103. 183 and 103. 200, seem to refer to trust property.   [15] *Ibid.* 108. 9.

Paternoster,[1] a tenement in Alder-Mary Church parish, and rents in St. Martin Orgar,[2] and he also held as a feoffee with his brother-in-law Vanner and three other men, two of whom were also vintners, a hospice with lands, wharf and "la crane called 'Picards crane'" and an advowson to a chantry in the church of St. Magnus, all within that parish.[3] Outside London he held at the time of his death in 1388, six manors in Kent [4] besides other land in that county,[5] three manors in Middlesex [6] and other land there, and real property in St. Albans.[7] Stock and other movables at six of these manors and on his property at Roxhithe and Harrow were valued after his death at £331 4s. 7d.[8] Anticipating his downfall he granted his brother-in-law Vanner and four other Londoners all his goods and chattels, a month before he was accused of treason by the Lords Appellant[9] so that we can only guess at the extent of these, but in spite of this grant we find 10 cloths of gold, valued at £40, forfeited by him to the Crown[10] as well as 35 tuns and a pipe of woad valued at £300 13s. 4d.[11]

Brembre is often called simply a merchant (mercator),[12] more often a grocer, sometimes a pepperer;[13] there are

---

[1] H.R. 115. 169. This had belonged to Dame Katherine de la Pole.

[2] Cal. Inquis. P.M. III, p. 124.   [3] H.R. 114. 86.

[4] Haneworth, Mereworth, Charles Roughille and Halewele (Cal. Inquis. P.M., p. 107) and Lewisham and Greenwich (Inquis. Misc. Chancery, 145, file 332).

[5] Cal. Inquis. P.M., p. 107.

[6] Northalle, Doune and Woxindon, ibid. p. 110.   [7] Ibid. p. 107.

[8] Cal. P.R. 1385-89, p. 478. The value of each article is given in detail, or rather the price which Brembre's widow paid for each to the king. He had goods also at the manor of Cresbroke in Cheshunt (Cal. Fine Rolls, 1383-91, p. 222).

[9] Cal. P. and M.R., 1381-1412, p. 134. He conveyed his lands and tenements to Vanner and a John Fitznichole the day before he was appealed. Guildhall Library, original deeds Add. MS. 36; cf. Nicholas Exton's action in 1375: Williams, Early Holborn, 1617-18, 1661-62.

[10] Extracts from the Issue Rolls, p. 235. De Vere at the same time forfeits only three cloths of gold, ibid.

[11] Cal. Fine Rolls, 1383-91, p. 224.   [12] H.R., passim.

[13] Cal. L.B.F, p. 287. The pepperers, canvas dealers and spicers had combined to form the fraternity of grocers in 1345. See Dr. Thrupp in Eng. Trade in 15th Cent., pp. 248-9.

records of his trading in iron, wines [1] and woad,[2] and above all in wool—though there appears to be only one occasion on which he is called a " Wolmongere."[3] He was mayor of the staple of Westminster from 24 December 1385 to 28 January 1388, succeeding Walworth at his death, and being removed from office at the time of his fall by a royal writ.[4] The business which he carried on through the staple was great enough for it to be worth while for him to rent a house at Westminster.

In the two years during his lifetime for which we have lists of merchants exporting wool and wool-fells from London, his exports take a high place. In 1380–81 he exported 286 sacks and 15½ cloves, out-distancing both Walworth and Philipot ; only two London merchants, two provincial merchants and one alien merchant exported more than he. In 1384–85 he exported 288½ sacks and 14½ cloves, three Londoners exporting more, but no alien or provincial.[5] In connection with this staple trade we also find Brembre nominating attorneys in Ireland.[6] He was in touch, naturally, with many foreign merchants, and on one occasion made himself useful to John of Gaunt by bringing to him at Bruges 500 marks from London.[7] Some idea of the extent of his business dealings with foreigners

[1] *Cal. P.R.*, 1370–74, pp. 176 and 181. In the first case he, W. Canynges, J. Stodeye and others shared a cargo in these two commodities coming from Bayonne, in the second the cargo was loaded at Plymouth on a Dartmouth ship and Robert Knolles had jewels on board. See also *Cal. Cl.R.* 1381–85, pp. 354–5.

[2] *Cal. Fine Rolls*, 1383–91, pp. 223–4 (at Salisbury) ; *Cal. Cl.R.* 1387–88, p. 362 (at Colchester).

[3] *Cal. L.B.G*, fo. cclxib.

[4] E. E. Rich, "The Mayor of the Staple," *Camb. Hist. Journal*, IV, pp. 192–3. For the other information about Brembre as a stapler I am indebted to Miss J. S. A. Macaulay, B.Litt., who lent me her unpublished thesis on the staple at Westminster in the reign of Richard II.

[5] Some of this wool was bought of a certain John Salmon of Notyngham of whom Miss Macaulay found a record that he had used false weights in a sale to Brembre. On the other hand, after Brembre's execution Salmon claimed that Brembre had bought 84½ sacks of wool from him promising to pay £591 10s. for them but that he had not paid him, although they had been taken to Middelburgh for sale (*Cal. Cl.R.* 1385–89, p. 400).

[6] *Cal. P.R.*, 28 March 1375–76, m. 29.

[7] *John of Gaunt's Register*, I, p. 79.

may be gained from the City records and elsewhere. He and John Pyel, mercer,[1] for example, gain possession in 1374 of property to the value of £1200 in connection with a certain Bartholomew Guidonis, a Lombard money-changer or financier ("lumbard chaungeor"), for whom Pyel and Brembre's father-in-law Stodeye had stood surety towards the Crown.   Brembre's part in this transaction may have been a subordinate one, and in 1378 it is with Philpot that he pays a Bruges merchant £2166 13s. 4d.[2] but later he himself becomes attorney for a merchant of Lucca ;[3] Luke Bragadyn, merchant of Venice, owed him £1250 in 1382 ;[4] he had dealings with two Bolognese merchants in 1384[5] and with Bragadyn again in 1385 ;[6] two other merchants of Lucca owed him £729 3s. 4d. in May 1383,[7] and one of these shared in a debt to him of 537 gold francs in the next month.[8] It was in this year apparently that Brembre and Vanner began lending money to sureties of the famous hostage Alfonso de Denia, in connection with whom had occurred the sensational violation of sanctuary at Westminster in 1378 ; and later they lent money to Denia himself and to Florimond, lord of Lesparre, with whom Denia was to be exchanged.[9] Brembre did not live to see this money repaid, nor yet the 800 marks he lent to the Portuguese ambassadors to England in 1384–85.[10]

    To Edward III's government Brembre, with a certain Thomas Albon,[11] lent £300, as part of a City loan in 1370–71,[12] and a further sum in 1374,[13] an unspecified share of £3000 with five others.

[1] H.R. 103. 24. 26. 27.

[2] Cal. P.R. 1377–81, p. 280. This was in connection with the war.

[3] Cal. P. and M.R. 1364–81, p. 204.

[4] Ibid. 1381–1412, p. 41. Bragadyn was exporting wool from the staple of Westminster in 1380–81 according to Miss Macaulay.

[5] Ibid. pp. 82 and 83.   [6] Ibid. p. 98.

[7] P.R.O. Lists and Indexes, xlix, no. 1361.

[8] Ibid. no. 302.

[9] Ibid. nos. 1346, 305, 306, 303a, 308, 307a, and see also Ed. Perroy, The Diplomatic Correspondence of Richard II, pp. 236–7.

[10] Ibid. p. 209.

[11] With whom he owned property in London in 1375 (H.R. 103. 57).

[12] Cal. L.B.G., p. 276.

[13] Cal. P.R. 10 December 1374, p. 36.

To Richard II's government, however, his loans are of far greater importance. The political significance of his relations with that king will be discussed in a later chapter; at the moment we are concerned with his wealth, and that was great enough to enable him to advance personally to Richard's government £2970 between 1377 and 1387, apart from his contributions to corporate loans from the City.[1]

The contrast between Brembre and his bitter opponent John de Northampton is striking in many ways. He is known by two surnames, Northampton or Norhampton, and Comberton or Cumberton, though usually by the former, while other members of his family are usually known by the latter. Both surnames are to be found in the City records. That of Northampton or Norhampton is of very common occurrence in the Hustings Rolls;[2] and though the use of the same place-name as a surname obviously does not prove kinship it seems likely that some at least of those mentioned were related to John. Of his two brothers mentioned in his will, William predeceased him,[3] probably by a good number of years; he was a skinner, and it was probably he who was imprisoned in 1365[4] for mixing old and new fur " against the statute and in deception of the people," and again in 1371[5] for resisting tax-collectors and making an affray outside the mayor's house. His brother Robert, who after John's arrest by Brembre in 1384, attempted to rescue him[6] by force of arms, and was himself

---

[1] A. Steel, " Eng. Govt. Finance, 1377–1413," in *E.H.R.*, October 1936, pp. 29–51. Mr. Steel's figures are from 1377–89, but Brembre was appealed of treason in November 1387 and tried in the following February so that in his case the period is shorter. Philipot, and Venour, also a grocer, both lent even more than Brembre.

[2] There seem to be thirteen distinct men of that name Londoners in the thirteenth century and fifteen in the fourteenth century. There does not seem to be any place called Comberton in Northamptonshire though such exist in Cambridgeshire, Herefordshire and Worcestershire, nor do the printed Records of the Borough of Northampton (2 vols. 1898) mention this name. The printed list of freemen, however, does not go back beyond 1561.

[3] *Cal. Wills Court of Hustings*, II, pp. 333–5. *Commiss. of Lond. Regist. Books, Courtenay*, fols. 406–7. See also *MS. Cal.* to *H.R.* 1432.

[4] *Cal. P. and M.R.* 1364–81, p. 15.

[5] *Ibid.* p. 134.   [6] See Appendix IV.

arrested and imprisoned was one of his executors ;[1] there is no record of Robert as belonging to any mistery, but in one place in the Hustings Rolls, he is called an esquire of London.[2] Northampton's mother and father are mentioned in his will, but only by their Christian names, Mariota and James.[3] He was twice married, but of his first wife Johanna, who was alive in 1371, we know nothing.[4] His second marriage, some time before 1375, was like Brembre's in that it brought him considerable wealth. It was to Petronilla, daughter and co-heiress of John de Preston, junior, who in his turn was heir of John de Preston, corder, and his brother Peter.[5] Petronilla was a widow with at least two daughters when Northampton married her,[6] and she can have had no children by him who survived her, for on her death we find Northampton retaining only a life interest in the estate, which was to devolve on his death to his step-daughter Idonia who was married to North- ampton's brother Robert.[7] Petronilla's mother was Margaret Costantyn or Constantyn,[8] and a member of that family, John Constantyn, cordwainer, was executed in 1384 for attempting to raise an insurrection four days after Northampton's arrest.[9]

[1] In the summary of the will in the Calendar mentioned above, his name is wrongly transcribed as " Roger " ; the relationship of William, Agnes, Petronilla, Johanna and John is not at all clear in this summary. They were all the children of Northampton's brother William.   [2] H.R. 125. 94 dors.

[3] A James Northampton, son of Robert, occurs earlier in the Hustings Rolls, in the fourteenth century. John de Northampton's son, to whom he left most of his property, is called James.

[4] H.R. 100. 21 : except that she was concerned, with her husband, in the purchase of a shop in St. Mary le Bow.

[5] Ibid. 124. 32. See also Cal. Wills, 1, pp. 435 and 669, for the wills of Petronilla's father and grandfather, dated 1339 and 1353 respectively. It is somewhat of a coincidence that her father should leave a chalice to " John de Northampton of the order of preachers."

[6] Cal. Cl.R. 1381-85, p. 494, where it speaks of them as having been in the wardship of the prioress of Kilburn. As Idonia is spoken of later as the " heiress " of John and Peter Preston, perhaps her sister (or sisters) died or entered religion.   [7] H.R. 124. 32.   [8] Cal. Wills, 1, p. 669.

[9] See Cal. L.B.H, p. 231. Cal. P. and M.R. 1381-1412, p. 50 and Appendix IV. His head remained upon Ludgate for four years till the time of Brembre's trial (Cal. Cl.R. 1387-88, p. 325. A William Costantyn was also among his supporters and seems also to have lost his life (Cal. P. and M.R. 1381-1412, p. 62),

It was through his marriage with Petronilla that Northampton acquired most of his property. Some of this was in the parish of St. Nicholas Flesh-Shambles,[1] some in the old Fish-market,[2] in Castle Baynard Ward, and some near the Steelyard by the Heywharf in Dowgate,[3] some in the parish of St. Martin, Ironmonger Lane,[4] some in that of St. Andrew within Newgate[5] and some in St. Owin's or St. Ewin's parish,[6] which was in Farringdon Ward within. In addition to all this he had first rented a shop and a warehouse lying next door to one another in the parish of St. Mary le Bow, Cordwainer Street Ward, and then bought the shop from Richard Norbury, mercer, later one of his most prominent supporters.[7] He later held a twenty years' lease of a corner shop in Cordwainer Street in the same parish[8] and a forty years' lease of two messuages and three shops, in the same street, these last belonging to the prioress and convent of Dartford.[9] The owner of the corner shop was another of his most prominent supporters, William Essex, draper, and it is possible that he may have been Northampton's partner at one time ; in any case he and John More, mercer (the third most prominent supporter of Northampton), and Thomas Baret, who is described as Northampton's apprentice, held lands and tenements in Pentecost Lane, St. Nicholas Shambles, from John and Petronilla Northampton from 30 November 1375 to 12 February 1376.[10] In Dowgate Ward Northampton bought a dyehouse and two adjoining tenements in

---

[1] In Farringdon Within (*P. and M.R.* 1381–1412, p. 239; *H.R.* 103. 283).
[2] *Cal. Cl.R.* 1381–85, pp. 501, 521, 628. *Cal. P.R.* 1381–85, p. 463.
[3] *Ibid.*   [4] *H.R.* 124. 32.   [5] *Ibid.*
[6] *Cal. P.R.* 1381–85, pp. 462–3. It was part of the Dowgate property which was known later as " Northampton's Inn with the Broad Gates," *ibid.* 1381–85, p. 516.
[7] *H.R.* 100. 21. Norbury had married the widow of John de Evenfeld from whom Northampton had earlier held the shop.
[8] *Ibid.* 108. 46, 109. 2.
[9] *Cal. Cl.R.* 1381–85, p. 484. This lease dated from 1375. Northampton was living in Cordwainer Street at the time of his arrest. See Appendix IV.
[10] *H.R.* 103. 283; 104. 20. Will. Essex and two of Northampton's less prominent supporters, Robert Ryseby and Richard Brendewode were, with Northampton and others, concerned in some trust property (*H.R.* 112. 51).

Wendegooslane in the Ropery,[1] a tenement and two mansion houses in Cosyn Lane in the Ropery, late the property of Richard Lyons,[2] other lands and tenements in the parish of All Hallows at the Hay in the Ropery,[3] and lands, tenement houses and shops, together with a quay (formerly the property of Bartholomew Frestlyng).[4] These purchases took place mainly, if not entirely, between the spring of 1380–81 and that of 1381–82.[5] It is possible that this, which has the appearance of a deliberate concentration of property in one district, may account for the election of Northampton as alderman of Dowgate Ward in March 1381–82.[6] He had formerly, from 1375[7]–77,[8] been alderman of Cordwainer Street Ward, another district in which he and his wife had property,[9] but for the last five years he had not held that office in any ward. That John de Preston, senior, had been alderman of Dowgate for the eighteen years before his death,[10] and that the same position had been held from 1352–77 by Bartholomew Frestlyng,[11] some of whose property in the ward had been bought by Northampton in February 1381–82, adds probability to this conjecture.

Perhaps a minute study of the Hustings Rolls would show that the office of alderman of a ward was usually held by a man who held a great deal, if not almost all, of the real property in that ward.[12] However this may be, it is

---

[1] *Cal. P.R.* 1381–85, pp. 462–3. (For the subsequent history of the Wendegooslane property and its ultimate absorption into the steelyard, see Kingsford in *London Topographical Record*, xi, pp. 55–6.) One tenement of Northampton's, at the corner " between the said lane & the great hall of Estlandia " was granted to Roger Siglem of Bohemia, esquire of the King (*Cal. P.R.* 1385–89, p. 15). See also *Cal. Fine R.* x, p. 310, where his property in Gover Lane is mentioned.   [2] *Ibid.* 1381–85, pp. 462–3.

[3] *H.R.* 109. 12.   [4] *Ibid.* 110. 84 and 95.

[5] The transactions recorded in the Hustings Rolls bear dates of this period, while the purchase of the property in Cosyn Lane must have taken place after une 1381, when Lyons was murdered, as the other parties to the conveyance τere Lyons's executors.   [6] *Cal. L.B.H*, p. 177.

[7] *Ibid.* p. 9.   [8] *Ibid.* p. 59.   [9] See above, p. 9.

[10] *Cal. L.B.E*, p. 146 ; Beaven, *Ald. of London*, i, p. 136.

[11] *Cal. L.B.F*, p. 247 ; *Cal. L.B.H*, p. 59.

[12] This cannot have been so always, as the only property which Brembre seems to have held in Bread Street Ward, of which he was alderman from 1372 (*Cal. L.B.G*, p. 327) to the period of annual elections, appears to have been held in trust and in any case not to have been acquired till 1375 (*H.R.* 103. 183).

not at all unlikely that Northampton had this aim in view when he possessed himself of so much property in Dowgate Ward, for (apart from the dyehouse, the warehouse and the quay), there seems no reason why his business should have been affected by the locality in which his property was situated. Perhaps he was anxious to consolidate his influence in another ward besides that of Cordwainer Street, where his policy seems, from subsequent events,[1] to have been popular, and of which his close supporter, John More, was elected alderman[2] at the same time as his own election in Dowgate.

Although it is obvious that Northampton's property in the City was considerable, even there its amount does not approach that of Brembre.[3] Outside the City of London he indisputably held only certain lands in Beverley, Yorkshire,[4] and the Manor of Shoreditch previously held by John, Lord Nevill,[5] though he may also have held land in Tottenham.[6] There are not many records which throw light on his business, which does not seem to have been of very wide extent. We know that he once nominated attorneys in Ireland,[7] but there is no trace of his owning ships[8] or even goods in the ships of others,[9] of being engaged in commercial

---

[1] See Appendix IV. [2] *Cal. L.B.H*, fo. cxi.

[3] Northampton's has been described in more detail because of the probable political connections of some of it. It amounted to over 90 tenements to the annual value of over £150 (M. M. Postan in " Credit in Mediaeval Trade," *Econ. Hist. Review*, 1928, p. 237). The Index to the Hustings Rolls (which contain records of conveyances and leases, not of law suits) shows 52 entries with Philpot as one of the principals, 51 with Walworth, 37 with Brembre, 18 with Northampton, 12 with Essex, 8 with Norbury and 7 with John More.

[4] *Cal. Cl.R.* 1377–81, p. 381. [5] *Cal. P.R.* 1381–85, p. 462.

[6] The entry on the Close Rolls looks as if this were trust property, for John More, Robert Cumberton and others hold the lands as well as he, *ibid.* 1381–85, p. 210, on the other hand a son John is mentioned in the Middx. Feet of Fines—of whom there is no mention in either of his wills or in any City record (*Cal. Cl.R.* 1381–85, p. 388; *Lond. Middx. Feet of Fines*, p. 104). [7] *Cal. P.R.* 1380, p. 497.

[8] As John Hadle (*Cal. Cl.R.* 1377–81, p. 36) and Will. Venour, grocer (*Ibid.* 1381–85, p. 383, and *Cal. P.R.* 1396–99, p. 158), probably, and as Richard Lyons vintner (*Cal. Cl.R.* 1369–74, p. 226) and John Philpot (*ibid.* 1381–85, p. 495), certainly did.

[9] Contrast not only Brembre but Fifide (mercer), Staundon and Warde (grocers), etc. (*ibid.* 1377–81, p. 23 and *Cal. P.R.* 1367–70, pp. 469–70).

transactions with foreign merchants (unless the John de Gildesburgh who owed him a clear debt of £80 at the time of his arrest be one),[1] or of journeying abroad on business. There are nowhere recorded any recognisances entered into by him or to benefit him, but we know that at the time of his arrest he owed certain citizens of Salisbury £186 6s. 8d., and was owed 40 marks by a goldsmith and a draper of London, £34 18s. 6d. by another London draper and £2 by a third ;[2] John Clopton, vintner of London, owed him £117 (in this record Northampton is called clothier),[3] the Abbot of Stratford owed him £20 5s., the Prior of Prestelsham £9 5s. and Geoffrey Greg taverner, £40.[4] Besides his debt to the citizens of Salisbury he owed a certain Agnes Hale £71 10s.[5] and £12 9s. 5d. to a blacksmith of London.[6] There is no trace of Northampton having exported wool from the staple of Westminster. It is difficult to establish with certainty what position in his mistery was held by him, because the earliest wardens accounts of the Drapers are for the year beginning in August 1413.[7] Further, though records of men being admitted masters of their craft and sworn wardens of their mistery often appear in the City Letter Books, the only record of the kind relating to Northampton is one of February 1360–61, in which he is mentioned as one of four " upholderes " of the drapers.[8] The absence of any such record in the Letter Books, however, does not prove that he was never master or warden, as the records of the goldsmiths testify in similar cases.[9]

The only sum which he is known for certain to have lent

---

[1] *Cal. P.R.* 1385–89, p. 60. [2] *Cal. Cl.R.* 1385–89, p. 17.
[3] *Ibid.* P.R. 1381–85, p. 456. [4] *Ibid.* p. 513.
[5] *Ibid.* p. 513.

[6] *Ibid. Cl.R.* 1385–89, p. 21. Contrast with these sums a debt of Brembre's at the time of his death, of £450 to Nicholas Exton and his wife, *Cal. P.R.* 1385–89, p. 478. There is a record of a debt of £32 to him in 1367, apparently from a vintner (*Cal. P. and M.R.* 1364–81, p. 70).

[7] A. H. Johnson, *History of the Worshipful Company of Drapers of London,* I, p. 283.

[8] *Cal. L.B.G,* p. 126. Another of the four was Thomas Noket, later one of his supporters (*C.R.R.,* p. 507).

[9] These which begin in 1332, are unprinted. See below, with reference to the followers of Northampton who were goldsmiths.

to the Crown is £76 13s. 4d. as part of that City loan of
£4621 13s. 4d. in 1370–71 mentioned above,[1] to which
Brembre and Albon contributed £300, Walworth, £233
6s. 8d. and Philpot £163 6s. 8d. He may, however, be the
John Northampton who lent the King £10 in 1369 ; [2]
and when, in 1379, the " good folk of the City " advanced
£600 to appease the lords and regain their custom,
Northampton contributed £4, Walworth and Brembre £5
each and Philpot £10.[3] This is the only occasion when he
appears in anything approaching the same financial rank
as Brembre.

Of the third class, that of small masters of the misteries,
there are many examples among Northampton's followers,
who will be discussed in a later chapter.

It is quite impossible to give an accurate number of
these misteries in 1376. Dr. A. H. Thomas,[4] for example,
refers to a list of crafts drawn up in 1422 by the brewers,
in which the number is 111, but adds that the " crafts of
London in the fourteenth and fifteenth centuries are seen
as in an ever-moving kaleidoscope—the coalescing of divers
misteries into one company and the breaking up of large
companies into separate misteries." There was often much
bitterness between the misteries, sometimes breaking out
into great violence as, for example, in 1373, when John
Northwold, mercer " at a wrestling " " was slain at the
black heath, where through arose a great dissension and
debate among the crafts of London." [5] There was a
particular " rancour " between the pepperers and the
goldsmiths which broke out notably one Sunday in March
1378.[6] The hostility between the victualling and non-
victualling misteries at this time was indeed of vital importance, though it was by no means so clear-cut an issue as it
has often been made to appear. Perhaps the most turbulent of
all the misteries was that of the fishmongers, who not only
quarrelled with other misteries[7] as on the occasion in 1373

[1] p. 6. Cal. L.B.G, p. 276.
[2] Devon, Issue Roll of Thomas de Brantingham, p. 145.
[3] Cal. L.B.H, p. 124.
[4] In his introduction to his Cal. P. and M.R. 1364–81, p. xxxvi.
[5] Harleian 565, ed. Nicholas, p. 69.
[6] Riley, Memorials, pp. 415–16, see below, pp. 68-9.
[7] Cal. P. and M.R. 1364–81, p. 151.

mentioned above, but very violently among themselves. [1]
The fishmongers were, indeed, in a unique position at that
time. Every other mistery was essentially under the
control of the mayor and aldermen, however much it
might in ordinary practice manage its own affairs. Even
the weavers, who had the oldest privileged craft in London,
and whose right to hold a court of their own was based on
a charter, had, since 1321, acknowledged the authority of
the City government. Although they had struggled to
maintain the independence of their court, particularly in
the first twenty years of the fourteenth century, they now
recognised an appeal from it to the Mayor's Court, and
no longer claimed the right of citing before it cases of debt
in which the defendant was not a weaver, even though the
plaintiff was.[2] The Court of the Fishmongers, on the other
hand, was so powerful that it has even been described as
a " seignuire collective comparable to the liberties of St.
Martin's and Blackfriars." [3] The right of the bailiff of their
" Halimoot " in Bridge Street to call any cases into it from
the City Courts if a fishmonger were involved had been
challenged at the Iter of 1321, when the weavers had lost
their power, but the fishmongers had triumphed and since
1365 had based their claims not only on prescription but
on charter.[4] By their very success they were bound to
incur unpopularity with their fellow-citizens but this in
any case they were likely to excite, as the provider of one
of the most important staple foods of the fourteenth century.
No privileges seem to have been dearer to the Londoner
of this period than the independence and authority of his
civic courts [5] and his right of not being forced to plead in

---

[1] *Cal. P. and M.R.*, pp. 27 and 35. See also a " great affray " between
the skinners and fishmongers in 1339-40 (*Cal. P. and M.R.* 1323-64, p.
107 ; Introd. pp. xxviii and xxix).

[2] F. Consitt, *The London Weavers' Coy.*, i, pp. 19, 25, 97, and Unwin,
Gilds and Companies, pp. 37-42.

[3] Unwin, *Gilds and Companies*, pp. 37-42.   [4] *Ibid.*

[5] For a description of the jurisdiction and procedure of the Mayor's
Court, the Court of Hustings and the Sheriff's Court and the distinctions
between them, see A. H. Thomas, *Introd. to Calendar of Early Mayor's Court
Rolls*, and below, Chapter III, p. 32 ; for criminal jurisdiction as exercised
by the mayor see the Charter granted by Edward III in 1327 (Birch : *Historical
Charters and Constitutional Documents of the City of London*, pp. 52-8).

any court outside the City. The action of anyone, whether the King or a subject, which attacked this privilege, met with bitter resentment, and often with violence ; further, while, for example, great jealousy was shown towards the Ecclesiastical Courts whose jurisdiction in many ways overlapped that of the City Courts, the attempts to extend the jurisdiction of the marshal [1] into the City seem to have united the Londoners as nothing else was able to unite them. On their part they claimed authority over Southwark, the seat of the Marshalsea, basing this claim on the charter of 1327 which had granted them that " vill " on their plea that it was a place of refuge for malefactors of the City,[2] especially for victuallers offending against City ordinances.

The jealousy of the Ecclesiastical Courts, the " Courts Christian," was not expressed so violently, but it was consistent, and of long standing. It was only in London and in towns, such as Oxford, whose liberties were based on those of London,[3] that any but Ecclesiastical Courts took cognisance of cases of usury [4] or slander [5] or the enrolment of wills.[6] In connection with this last point we have evidence of the jealousy with which the City guarded the special privileges of its courts in the record of the loss of his freedom from 1370–74 by the Richard Norbury mentioned above,[7]

---

[1] See *Collected Papers* of T. F. Tout, II, pp. 153–4 and 229–30, for limitations on the Steward's and Marshal's Courts which illustrate the suspicion with which they were regarded in general. London, of course, was in a particularly difficult position, as it was within the verge, as usually interpreted, when the King was in residence at Westminster (see *Rot. Parl.* II, pp. 336–7, III, p. 267, for the extent of the verge and *ibid.* II, p. 441, for London's grievance) and he was increasingly so in the last 28 years of Edward III ; T. F. Tout, *Collected Papers*, III, p. 264.

[2] Birch, *Hist. Charters*, pp. 59–60. There was a marshalsea of the household and another of the King's Bench, both built since 1372, and used as prisons as well as courts (T. F. Tout, *Collected Papers*, III, pp. 272–3).

[3] Sharpe, *Cal. of Wills*, I, pp. vi–vii, and Thomas, *Introd. Cal. P. and M.R. 1323–64*, p. xxxvi.

[4] *Cal. L.B.G*, pp. 160–1, 162, and 267.

[5] *Cal. L.B.G*, pp. 176–7, *Memorials*, pp. 385–6, *Cal. L.B.H*, pp. 94 and 134. MS. Files of Actions of Mayor's Court Rolls E.III and R.II, nos. 122, cf. *Cal. L.B.C*, p. 18, and *Cal. L.B.G*, p. 283.

[6] This the City had practised since 1258, see Sharpe, *Cal. of Wills* enrolled in the Court of Husting.   [7] p. 9.

for appealing to the Courts Christian in a matter touching the will of his wife's late husband, John de Evenfeld, which had been proved in the Husting Court.[1] The same detestation of outside interference was to be seen seventeen years later in the imprisonment of certain serving men of the mistery of the cordwainers for attempting to get from the Pope, through a certain Dominican, a confirmation of their own serving-men fraternity which held its meetings in the house of the Black Friars,[2] " a deed," says the contemporary clerk, " which notoriously redounds to the weakening of the liberties of the . . . City, and of the power of the officers of the same." [3] With this may be compared the action brought in 1344 against the pouchers, by a member of that craft, because they administered to all their members, in a Court Christian, an oath not to sell goods below a certain price, the oath being declared to be contrary to the ordinances of the City.[4]

London's privileges were liable to be called in question at moments of national crisis, while the close connection of her most prominent citizens with the Government often made their position precarious at such moments. The meeting of the " Good " Parliament in 1376 was such an occasion, and important changes in London resulted from that Parliament.

[1] *Cal. L.B.G*, pp. 262–3.   [2] *Cal. L.B.H*, p. 311.
[3] *Memorials*, p. 496.
[4] *Cal. P. and M.R.* 1323–64, pp. 159–60 and 211. As early as 1292 an action was heard in the Mayor's Court against a monk of Westminster who had impleaded a citizen for trespass in a Church Court outside the City walls, and who brought two Papal Bulls to support what he had done as being lawful by reason of his privileges from the Roman see, *Cal. L.B.A*, p. 144, quoted by Dr. Thomas in his introduction to the *Cal. Early Mayor's Courts Rolls*, p. xx.

The case of a woman, in 1377, bound over to abandon proceedings in a Court Christian for slander, against some Wardemote jurors, is also of interest in this connection (*Cal. P. and M.R.* 1364–81, p. 244), see also *Memorials*, pp. 462–3, for a case in which sorcery and slander are both concerned.

CHAPTER II

THE "GOOD" PARLIAMENT AND LONDON

THE year 1376 was the starting point of constitutional experiments in London which will be described in the next chapter, while in that year and in the early part of 1377 occurred a series of events which are very significant in view of the future development of parties in London, and which furnish what is perhaps the only key to John of Gaunt's relations with the City and subsequent connection with John of Northampton.

The "Good" Parliament sat from 28 April[1] to 6 July,[2] 1376, and it was almost certainly while it was sitting that the leaders of the party in London which desired annual election of aldermen and a change in the method of electing the Common Council[3]—that is to say by misteries instead of by wards—succeeded in getting government support for their schemes. It is true that the charter declaring that aldermen must be re-elected only after a year's interval was not issued till 12 November,[4] but the Letters of Privy Seal threatening intervention in the Common Council question are dated as early as 29 July.[5] The fact, however, which links most closely City affairs with the proceedings of the "Good" Parliament is that the assembly of the mayors, the recorder, the sheriffs, nine of the remaining aldermen,[6] and commoners from forty-one misteries, which met on

[1] *Rot. Parl.* ii, p. 321. [2] *Ibid.* p. 360.

[3] If, indeed, the assemblies before 1376 can be given the same title as those after it. See below, Chapter III, p. 36.

[4] *Cal. L.B.H*, p. 58, note 2. [5] *Ibid.* p. 35.

[6] The mayor, the recorder and one of the sheriffs were also aldermen. It is curious that two of the nine, Adam St. Ives and Hervey Begge were, strictly speaking, elected till 4 August, in the place of Pecche and Bury, discharged at this council at which St. Ives and Begge are mentioned as having been present as aldermen. Richard Lyons, the third discharged alderman, was succeeded by John Organ, whose presence is not recorded.

1 August, to change the method of electing common councillors, met also to degrade from the office of alderman those London citizens who had been impeached in the " Good " Parliament.[1]

This assembly was summoned by the mayor, John Warde,[2] who was afterwards, curiously enough, one of Lyons's executors and legatees, with the advice of John of Northampton,[3] Adam Stable,[4] Nicholas Twyford[5] and two other aldermen,[6] together with eight commoners, five of whom were Northampton's followers.[7] The avowed object of the council was to find remedy for the grievances put forward by a petition of the commonalty through the Common Serjeant ; these grievances were—first " the great slander " raised in the late Parliament against the City because of the misbehaviour " of which some persons had been convicted in full Parliament and others were still under great suspicion," and, secondly, the oppressive and unjust manner in which the mayor and aldermen had, of late, governed the City for their own profit. The " persons convicted in full Parliament " were Richard Lyons, vintner, alderman of Broad Street since 1374[8] and sheriff in that year.[9] Adam de Bury, skinner, alderman of Langbourn since 1349,[10] sheriff in that year[11] and mayor from 1364–66[12] and again in 1373,[13] and John Pecche, fishmonger, alderman of Walbrook since 1349,[14] sheriff in 1352[15] and mayor in 1361.[16] We do not know the names of those who " were still under great suspicion." It is almost certain that John Pyel, mercer, was one of them[17] and it is significant that he is

---

[1] *Cal. L.B.H*, pp. 38–41.   [2] Grocer.
[3] Draper.   [4] Mercer.   [5] Goldsmith.
[6] John Fifhide, mercer, and John Chichester, goldsmith.
[7] R. Norbury, J. More, W. Essex, R. Fraunceys and J. Willarby. *Cal. L.B.H*, p. 38.
[8] *Cal. L.B.G*, p. 322.   [9] *Ibid.* p. 326.
[10] Beaven, *Aldermen*, I, p. 167.   [11] *Cal. L.B.F*, p. 204.
[12] *Cal. L.B.G*, pp. 175, 203.   [13] *Ibid.* p. 312.
[14] Beaven, *Aldermen*, I, p. 216.   [15] *Cal. L.B.F*, p. 286.
[16] *Ibid.* p 287.
[17] See Dr. Galbraith's comment in his edition of the *Anominalle Chronicle*, p. 182, and pp. 86 and 89 of the chronicle itself in that edition. Pyel had been concerned in many loans to the king : notably he had been attorney for a group of men who were lending money to enable the king to pay off his

one of ten aldermen who did not attend the meeting of
1 August. It is very possible that others of the absentees
were under suspicion too. They included William Walworth
and three other fishmongers,[1] John Stodeye, vintner,[2]
John Philpot and Nicholas Brembre and one other grocer [3]
and John de Chichester, goldsmith. Their absence from the
meeting is difficult to account for in any other way, as is
the complete absence of any recorded opposition to the
changes brought about at this time, changes which some
of these men were afterwards to reverse,[4] which struck at
the monopoly of government possessed by the existing court
of aldermen, and whose discussion had earlier caused such
dissensions in the City.[5] Not only Pyel, but nearly all the
aldermen who were absent from the meeting of 1 August
belonged, too, to the same class as Lyons, Pecche and
Bury, the class of merchant capitalists who advanced money
to the Government and held office under it [6]—more particularly office connected with the Customs or the Mint—a
class peculiarly liable to attack from economising knights
of the shire and from lesser merchants, especially those
of their own City. The lack of support of the three accused
aldermen by any section of the Londoners does not necessarily

debt to the Bardi and again with Lyons for the loan in 1374, although he
denied the fact (*Cal. P.R.* 1370–74, p. 196 and *ibid.* 1374–77, p. 5), while
he had been the king's envoy beyond the sea (*Cal. P.R.* 1358–61, p. 433)
and deputy changer of the king's money (*Cal. Cl.R.* 1349–54, p. 378) and
summoned to the king's Council in 1357 (*Rot. Parl.* ii, pp. 456–7). He
and Adam Fraunceys had business dealings with Alice Perrers in January
1370–71 (*Cal. P.R.* 1370–74, p. 50).

[1] John Wroth, John Little and John Tornegold.   [2] See above, p. 2.
[3] John Aubrey.   [4] *Cal. L.B.H*, pp. 156, 227 and 228.
[5] *Ibid.* p. 35. The annual election of aldermen was not settled till
November, but it is evidently part of the same policy.
[6] J. Chichester, goldsmith, had been master of the king's money from
1351–55 (*Cal. Cl.R.* 1349–54, p. 313, and 1354–60, p. 235), had lent the
king money in 1370 (*Cal. L.B.G*, p. 275) and was possibly keeper of the Prince
of Wales' Wardrobe (*ibid.* p. 291), see *Rot. Parl.* iii, p. 9, for a later
petition against him and other rich goldsmiths by Will. Fitzhugh because
of an alleged forcing by them of their poorer companions to agree not to sell
under very high prices—with an implication that the poorer men could
thereby get no sale. For Brembre see above, pp. 6–7. Note particularly his
connection with Pyel, *H.R.* 103. 24, 26, 27. For Walworth and Philpot
see *D.N.B.*

tell against this theory, that the absence of opposition to the constitutional changes was due to the fear of those who would naturally have led such an opposition that they would thereby be involved in the ruin of their fellow aldermen ; on the contrary, it supports it. The accusations against Lyons were, first, that he had used his position as collector of the wool subsidy and member of the king's Council to export wool elsewhere than to the staple at Calais; that he had imposed duties without consent of Parliament and had appropriated some of the issues to his own use; that he had employed " usury " in his loans to the king, and, finally, that he had bought up cheaply the loans of others to the king, securing for himself, later, full payment out of the Treasury.[1] Adam de Bury was impeached for deceit practised on the king while he was mayor of Calais and Captain of Balyngeham ;[2] he never appeared to answer his accusers, so that the charge against him is not given in detail ; his non-appearance, however, is significant, particularly as his earlier record was not a particularly good one : he had been discharged from the office of mayor in January 1365–66,[3] while in April 1367 he had found it worth while to obtain a pardon for the death of a certain skinner, for sedition and for frauds touching the exchange of the king's money.[4] The accusation against John Pecche was that he had purchased a monopoly of the sale of sweet wines in the City and that he had used this monopoly to levy a so-called duty on all the wine sold, thereby increasing its price.[5] It was declared in the articles of impeachment that the monopoly was to the " destruction of the Franchise

[1] *Rot. Parl.* II, p. 323. In the *Anominalle Chronicle* (p. 89), on being questioned by the Duke of Lancaster, Walworth declared that he did not make the " chevauns," but that Richard Lyons and John Pyel did—a fact which Pyel successfully, if not truthfully, denied. Earlier the assertion had been made that the king could have borrowed from Walworth and Adam Fraunceys at a far cheaper rate than from Lyons. It is noteworthy that in his reply to John of Gaunt, Walworth does not say that he (with Brembre, Brembre's brother-in-law Birlyngham and three other Londoners) had lent the king £3,000. In the arrangement made for their repayment, 10 December 1374, it was stipulated that Lyons and Pyel were to be paid first (*Cal. P.R. 1374–78*, p. 56).

[2] *Ibid.* p. 330.   [3] *Cal. L.B.G,* p. 205.
[4] *Cal. P.R. 1364–67*, p. 391.   [5] *Rot. Parl.* II, p. 328.

of the city too." [1] Now both Lyons and Pecche, in their
defence, attempted to shift some of the responsibility for
their doings on to their fellow-citizens and their fellow
aldermen in particular ; they both failed. Lyons acknowledged only one of the accusations against him to be true—
that of the imposition on wool—and this he declared to
have been placed by command of the king, and by the
petition and assent of the merchant class ; the king, however,
denied having given such an order, and the merchants did
not come forward in his defence. [2] John Pecche, for his
part, declared that the duty he had levied on sweet wines
had been agreed upon after consultation with, and with the
consent of, the mayor and certain aldermen, [3] whom he
named ; [4] when questioned in Parliament, however, the
mayor and aldermen utterly denied all responsibility or
share in the matter, [5] though it is extremely probable that
what Pecche said was true. [6] In a very similar fashion
Brembre, at his trial in the " Merciless " Parliament nearly
twelve years later, was left to his fate by those who had
supported him when mayor and were to continue his
civic policy, even though they were given an opportunity
of defending him. [7] The natural conclusion to draw is that

[1] *Rot. Parl.* II, p. 328.   It was no doubt on account of this that at this
time the ordinance was repealed which forbade the sale of sweet wines in
London and elsewhere and a declaration made that every freeman of the City
should be able to sell them retail or wholesale, but that the retail price
should be fixed by the mayor, as were the retail prices of other victuals,
ibid. II, p. 323.

[2] *Ibid.* p. 324.   When Lord Latimer was impeached, Walworth, one of the
London M.P.s, actually bore witness against him (*ibid.* p. 326), and see
above, p. 18.

[3] *Ibid.* p. 328.

[4] *Cal. L.B.H*, p. 40.   They were J. Warde, W. Halden, J. Chichestre,
J. Pyel, W. Walworth, J. Philpot, N. Brembre, J. Fyfhids, A. Stable, J. Little,
J. Hadle, B. Frestlyng, R. Hatfeld, J. Northampton, N. Twyford and J.
Maryns.

[5] *Rot. Parl.* p. 328.

[6] See *Cal. L.B.G*, pp. 192, 199 and 318.   The second of these entries refers
to a lease by Adam de Bury, mayor, the aldermen and the commonalty of
three taverns for sweet wines, in 1365, and the fixing of the price of the
different kinds of wine.   Halden, Chichestre, Little and Frestlyng were aldermen in this year.

[7] Higden, IX, p. 168.

an ever present fear of disturbance and dislike of outside interference led the wealthier citizens of London, all through this period, to support the apparently winning side in politics whenever this was possible, particularly when there existed internal divisions in the City at the same time, though these might be, and usually were, on different questions from those which agitated Parliament. Another fact supports this solution. A petition was put forward in the "Good" Parliament, by the mayor, aldermen and commonalty of the City, that merchant strangers [1] should not be allowed to sell by retail or to other strangers, to keep inns or to act as brokers.[2] This petition embodies the policy so soon afterwards to be bitterly opposed by John of Northampton, and as vehemently championed by Brembre and other victuallers, particularly the fishmongers. What is of importance, however, in connection with the question just discussed, is that the petition is only granted "on condition that they put the said City under good government to his honour [3] and to the profit of his kingdom" [4]— a phrase in which Londoners might well have seen a threat that the City might be "taken into the king's hand" [5] if it pursued a policy which did not please the party in power. No such comment was added when a similar petition was granted in Richard II's first Parliament.[6]

The fact that the petition was granted at all may show that John of Northampton and his party had not yet begun to formulate their policy against the victuallers, or that, even if he had done so, that Parliament was not interested

---

[1] The word used means aliens, not Englishmen, non-freemen of the City.

[2] *Rot. Parl.* II, p. 347.　　　　　　　　　　[3] i.e. the king.

[4] *Ibid.* (A clause follows guarding the privileges of the Hansa merchants.) The risk involved in loans to the Crown in the fourteenth and fifteenth centuries is shown in Mr. A. Steel's articles on English Government Finance 1377–1413 (*E.H.R.* 1936, pp. 29–51 and 577–97) together with the legal prohibition of interest made it almost impossible for any creditor of the Crown, however honest, to escape the imputation of "usury" if his financial dealings were examined by Parliament. This is probably the personal reason for the line of action of such a man as Walworth.

[5] This process involved the suspension of all the privileges of the City. See below, pp. 102–3.

[6] *Rot. Parl.* III, p. 27. On this occasion it is the privileges of the merchants of Aquitaine that are protected, not those of the Hansa merchants.

in what divided the parties in London, but only in the assistance this division gave it in attacking those whom it considered to be responsible for the bad state of the king's finances. This alternative is the more probable ; but however it may be, it is certain that at this moment there was no reason for John of Gaunt—later so decidedly Northampton's patron—to feel any gratitude towards him, or inclination to support him. In ousting Lyons, Pecche and Bury from their office as aldermen,[1] and, a few days later, depriving Pecche of the franchise of the City,[2] Northampton's party was doing all it could to support those who had attacked the duke's administration in Parliament ;[3] on the other hand he would naturally be drawn towards the opposing party which both would and could lend large sums of money to the crown—and to himself[4]—whereas there is no certain record of Northampton or his followers ever lending the king any money except where they were forced to share in a general City loan. The greater number of them do not even do this, which is a proof of their financial insignificance.[5]

The action of the duke when he again was in power supports this view. The Parliament which was to confirm by implication John of Gaunt's reversal of the policy of the " Good " Parliament met on 27 January[6] and sat till

[1] *Cal. L.B.H*, p. 38.

[2] *Ibid.* p. 44. (Lyons had been already condemned by Parliament to lose his.)

[3] W. Essex, one of the City M.P.s, was one of Northampton's closest followers, but Walworth and Karlille (a grocer), and probably Pyel, were opposed to his policy. It is of interest that although Pyel belonged to a " non-victualling " gild, that of the mercers, he had dealt on occasion in wheat, which he bought in Nottinghamshire and Sussex and sold in London (*Cal. P.R.* 1367–70, pp. 363 and 369).

[4] In December 1376 the Duke repaid £100 to John Philpot (D. L. Accs. various, Bundle III, No. 1). This entry is on the same roll as a payment of 100s. to Chaucer as an annuity.

[5] Mr. G. J. de C. Mead, in an unprinted London thesis on the " Financial Relations between the Crown and the City of London," shows that, at any rate under Edward III, a corporate City loan resulted in the poorer citizens being forced to subscribe more in proportion than the wealthier.

[6] *Rot. Parl.* II, p. 361.

23 February[1] 1376–77.[2] In it the Commons petitioned for the pardon of Lyons and Bury, among others condemned in the preceding Parliament, while John Pecche petitioned for his own pardon [3]—giving as a reason that judgment had been passed "without regular trial and by a hurried trial." No answer was given to these petitions in Parliament itself, as they had only been presented on the last day of the Session, but all three Londoners had obtained their pardons by 20 April—Lyons as early as 17 March.[4] There is no trace, however, of the City having re-admitted any of them to the franchise; certainly none of them ever held civic office again.[5]

It is not probable, however, that this failure to re-instate Lyons, Pecche and Bury was more than a small factor in the bitterness which now existed between the City and John of Gaunt, which culminated in the deposition of the mayor, Adam Stable, mercer, by order of the king, on 21 March 1376–77, and the election of Nicholas Brembre in his place, on the same day.[6] This incident is ascribed by the writer of the *Chronicon Angliae* to John of Gaunt's influence,[7] and at first sight it looks as if he were merely striking at the party which had opposed him the previous summer, or revenging himself on those Londoners who had lately seized the opportunity given them by Wiclif's trial at St. Paul's to riot and to insult him.[8] On closer examination, however, it beomes clear that it is not one party, but the

[1] *Rot. Parl.* II, p. 374.

[2] None of the City members was a supporter of Northampton, while one of his bitterest enemies, Nicholas Exton, fishmonger, sat for Middlesex (Return of M.P.s, Part I, p. 196).

[3] *Rot. Parl.* II, pp. 374–5.

[4] *Cal. P.R.* 1374–77, pp. 439, 453 and 457. It is mentioned that all Lyons's confiscated lands were restored to him: some of these had already been granted out to the Earl of Cambridge (*Cal. P.R.* 1374–77, p. 297) and others to Thomas of Woodstock and John of Gaunt's friend John of Ipre (*ibid.* 298).

[5] For their subsequent history see below, pp. 28–9.

[6] *Cal. L.B.H*, pp. 60–1.

[7] *Chron. Ang.* (R.S.), p. 398. The chronicle declares that the aldermen were all deposed as well—being misled probably by the annual elections which had just come into force. These elections took place in March.

[8] *Ibid.* pp. 118 ff.

whole City which is against the duke—united by fear of
the plans being made by John of Gaunt, Thomas of Woodstock and Henry Percy [1] to extend the marshal's jurisdiction
over the City.[2] The proposal to give the marshal power
to make arrests in the City was made on the morning of
19 February ; it was the afternoon of the same day that
Percy and John of Gaunt accompanied Wiclif to his trial
at St. Paul's. A riot followed, because of the rumour that
the marshal already had a prisoner in his London house.
John of Gaunt's palace of the Savoy was attacked,[3] as well
as Percy's house,[4] and there seems to have been a threat to
kill the latter. On its side the City was at this time
unsuccessfully attempting to extend its own jurisdiction
over Southwark, because of the alleged escape thither of
felons and those who broke the ordinances of the City,
and to do away with the marshal's jurisdiction there.[5]
In addition to his support of Percy, the duke seems to have
been planning that London should be " taken into the
king's hand " and that a " captain " should be appointed
instead of the mayor.[6] Perhaps Stable's deposition was
a substitute for the more drastic scheme ; but if John of
Gaunt hoped that the change of mayor would alter London's
attitude towards him and his plans he must have been
disappointed. The leader of the Londoners against him,

[1] Now Earl Marshal in the place of the Earl of March, *ibid.* p. 108.

[2] *Ibid.* p. 121. There had been a general petition in the Parliament which
was just closing against the wide extension of the jurisdiction of the Seneschal
and Marshal (*Rot. Parl.* II, pp. 366-7).

[3] *Chron. Ang.* p. 120.

[4] *Harleian* 565, pp. 70-1, where the prisoner is called " oon Prentyng
of Norfolk." The *Anominalle Chronicle* calls him John, Prentig of Norwich,
and says he was taken from the Earl Marshal's house to Newgate, and that
his imprisonment was due to the remarks he had made about John of Gaunt.
It also declares that the duke's coat of arms was reversed and that declarations
were made that he was the child of a butcher of Ghent, imposed on Edward
III when his real son died in infancy. As a form of apology, according to the
same chronicle, the mayor and aldermen in procession presented a candle,
and an escutcheon of the duke's, before Our Lady's image in St. Paul's,
the " comunes " refusing to take part (pp. 104-6). No doubt the governing
body of the City was more tactful than the mass of the citizens, but there is
no sign in the City Records of the strife between them on the subject which
is spoken of by the chronicler (p. 106).

[5] *Rot. Parl.* II, pp. 366-7.   [6] *Chron. Ang.* p. 120.

both before and after the deposition of Stable, was John Philpot[1] with whom the mayor, Brembre, was in close alliance.[2] Although the City authorities denied all responsibility[3] for the incidents of 19 February and even apologised for the disrespect shown to the duke,[4] they had left all attempt to control the riot to their bishop.[5] This then marks the break between John of Gaunt and the London capitalists. Never again is there any political alliance[6] between them; with the beginning of the new reign they form one of the strongest supports—if not the strongest of all—of the young King's Council at the time when Gaunt had no influence over it.

When the alliance began between the duke and John of Northampton is not so clear. It may have been in February 1377; for the reason why five men,[7] who were among Northampton's strong supporters, were removed from the Common Council in May 1377 was not only that they betrayed its secrets, but also that they had failed to support their fellow-citizens on the question of the Marshal's jurisdiction.[8] On the other hand Northampton himself, who was one of the sheriffs at the time,[9] is never once accused of such a thing. An alternative is that John of Gaunt saw his chance to form a party favourable to himself in London at the Parliament of Gloucester in 1378, of which Northampton was a member[10] and in which the fishmongers' monopoly was attacked; or the alliance may date from the autumn of 1381, when John of Northampton became mayor for the first time,[11] and when John of Gaunt was realising

---

[1] *Chron. Ang.* p. 120.   [2] See above, p. 2.

[3] *Chron. Ang.* p. 128.   [4] See above, p. 25, n.

[5] *Ibid.* p. 125. Courtenay seems to have been very popular in London, see *Anom. Chron.*, pp. 104–6 and *Vict. County History of London*, p. 212.

[6] Philpot, however, continued to lend the Duke money: he and the Earl of Arundel lent him 500 marks in 1379, and he sold him £100 worth of wine the same year. (Abstract of Reg. of J. Duke of Lancaster Temp. RII. In MS.)

[7] Will. Essex, John More, Richard Norbury, John Willoughby (or Willarby) and Robert Fraunceys.

[8] *Cal. L.B.H*, fo. lxi. This point about the Marshal is not mentioned in the précis of the passage given by Dr. Sharpe (*Cal. L.B.H*, p. 64).

[9] Chosen by the late mayor, John Warde. *Ibid.* p. 47.

[10] *Ibid.* p. 98.   [11] *Ibid.* p. 169.

to the full—after the sack of the Savoy in June—how unpopular he was in London. Of positive evidence, however, there is none, except that which concerns Northampton's followers, mentioned above. Northampton's appeal to the duke and the duke's response at the time of the ex-mayor's trial in the spring of 1384, point to a well-established connection between them,[1] but of any earlier connection no record whatever has survived, either in the duke's own accounts and registers,[2] in the Patent[3] or Close or Fine Rolls, or even in the Chronicles. A further difficulty is that it is impossible to date with accuracy the time when those who were later undoubtedly Northampton's followers began to be in close association with him,[4] though it is most likely that it was in 1376, or soon after. It was certainly just at this time, between the "Good" Parliament and the death of Edward III the following June, that the leadership in the party later opposed to Northampton passed from the older to the younger generation. This party has often been described as the "victualling party," but a more accurate name is the party of merchant capitalists, though it is true that most of them belonged to one or other of the great victualling misteries and that the monopoly of the fishmongers was one of the greatest points of controversy between them and their opponents.[5] Of the three most prominent leaders from 1377 onwards, William Walworth only had already been mayor ;[6] he had been elected alderman of Bridge on the death of his master John Lovekyn[7] in 1368, succeeding at the same time, so

---

[1] See below, Chapter V.

[2] These, unfortunately, have not all survived. The registers, however, cover the years 1372–76 and 1379–83, while there are accounts for 1376–77, 1392–93 and 1393–94. The names of many London citizens do occur in them.

[3] The only allusion here to any earlier connection, and that not a very illuminating one, is a pardon granted in November 1378 to Northampton's follower Robert Fraunceys, who was guilty of murder or at least homicide, " at the supplication of " the Duke of Lancaster (*Cal. P.R.* 1377–78, p. 297).

[4] Apart from his business association with some of them, see above, p. 9.

[5] This is the aspect of the struggle which seems to have survived in London tradition : see *Harleian* 565, p. 75 (this chronicle was probably written in 1442, in London). " Also in this yere (1382–83) fill debate in London betwen John Northampton, William Essex, John Moore, and Richard Norbury on that on partye, and the fysshmongers on the othere partye."

[6] In 1374 *Cal. L.B.G*, p. 327.   [7] *Ibid.* p. 234.

it appears, to Lovekyn's business ; [1] he had been sheriff in
1370.[2] John Philpot had been alderman of Cornhill since
1372 and Nicholas Brembre alderman of Bread Street for
the same length of time, both being elected alderman and
sheriff on the same day.[3] Their connection with each other
and with John Stodeye, who died in the autumn of 1376,
has been described already.[4] Stodeye's death removed
perhaps the greatest of the older capitalists ; of the others,
John Pyel, although he did not die till 1382,[5] ceased to take
any active part in City affairs after 1378, the last year in
which he served as alderman,[6] and the year in which he
made his will. (He had held a " seignurie " of John of
Gaunt in Northamptonshire, and we find the duke forbidding
his own servants to purvey any of Pyel's possessions.[7])
Another tenant of John of Gaunt, John Pecche,[8] was never
again prominent after his impeachment, and died three
years later.[9] Adam de Bury lived till the end of 1385,[10]
all through the stormy period of Northampton's mayoralty
and fall, but took no share whatever either in these matters
or in the financial relations of the City with the Crown.
Perhaps he lived in Calais, where he had property ; [11] the
Londoners had complained in 1376 of his long absences
from the City.[12] Lyons once more advanced the Crown
money[13] in 1379, the year in which he made his will ; in
1381 he met his death at the hands of the mob in the
Risings of that summer.[14] A fifteenth-century chronicle [15]
phrases it as follows : " And Richard Lyons and many
more of the Flemings were beheaded in divers places of

---

[1] *Harl.* pp. 565, 88–9.   See also *Cal. Wills*, II, p. 118.
[2] *Cal. L.B.G*, p. 265.   [3] *Ibid.* pp. 297–8.
[4] See above, p. 2.   [5] *Cal. Wills*, II, p. 228.
[6] *Cal. L.B.H*, p. 88.
[7] Armitage Smith : John of Gaunt's Register 1372–76, Entry no. 1374.
[8] *Ibid.* no. 1396.
[9] In accordance with his will his widow sold to John of Gaunt the lease
of a certain tenement in Lumbard Street (*Cal. Cl.R.* 1377–78, p. 461).
[10] *Cal. Wills*, II, p. 254.   [11] *Ibid.*
[12] *Cal. L.B.H*, p. 39.
[13] *Cal. P.R.* 1377–81, p. 637.   It is a possibility that this is not the same
man.
[14] *Memorials*, p. 450 ; *Cal. P.R.* 1381–85, p. 26.
[15] *Gregory's Chronicle* (Camden Soc.), p. 91.

London." The date of the Chronicle [1] is late, but it may be that Lyons was a foreigner, as his name seems to imply. The fact that he was a bastard [2] may account for the absence of family connections in the City, though he does not even seem to have married into one of the prominent City families ; [3] his official connection with the City, too, had only begun two years before the "Good" Parliament met, when he became alderman for Broad Street, and sheriff.[4]

Walworth, Philpot and Brembre, then, were from 1377 onwards the leaders of the capitalist party ; in that party there begin, about this time, to appear fresh names, the names of those who are to be the leading citizens of London at the end of the century—Exton, Karlille, Venour, Frossh, Hadle, St. Ives, and a little later, Hende, Barentyn, Whittington and Knolles. Opposed to this party stand Nicholas Twyford and Adam Bamme, as well as that section of the citizens who owned Northampton as leader, which will be described in a later chapter.[5]

[1] Probably 1469.

[2] *Cal. P. and M.R.* 1381–1412, p. 104. See also *Cal. P.R.* 1381–85, p. 52.

[3] Evidence for the marriage connections of the Londoners of this period abounds in the City records, owing to their peculiar customs concerning wills and orphans. A long law-suit, of whose final issue we have no record, took place between a woman named Isabella Pledour claiming to be Lyons's widow, and therefore entitled to half his goods, because he had died without children, and his executors, who declared that Isabella's marriage with Lyons had been annulled (*Cal. L.B.H*, p. 389; *Cal. P. and M.R.* pp. 151–3 and 184–5).

[4] *Cal. L.B.G*, pp. 322 and 327. He was, however, in London in 1364, when we find him bound over to keep the peace with Alice Perrers (*P. and M.R.* A 10m. 4d. (not calendared).

[5] Twyford and Bamme possessed much more wealth than most of Northampton's followers. Twyford can never be called one of these, though he was often in opposition to Brembre and Exton. Bamme, though favouring Northampton at first, seems finally to have thrown in his lot with the capitalist party. See below, Chapter V.

CHAPTER III

CONSTITUTIONAL CHANGES IN THE CITY
1376-97

THE constitutional history of the City of London during the twenty years 1376-97 is the history of an attempt so to change the forms of the constitution that the monopoly of political power held by a small number of wealthy men might be broken. These changes in form, though successfully carried out, failed to effect the desired result ; but they had given rise to such opportunities of friction and violence, between classes and between misteries, that the victorious capitalist party reversed them—actuated probably also by the fear that they might be of effective use in the future—and substituted a system in some ways even more favourable to an oligarchy than that which had existed before the conflict began.

Three changes were made in 1376. One, that of the annual election of aldermen, may perhaps at first sight be regarded as a return to ancient usage. By his charter of 1319 Edward II had granted to the Londoners that the aldermen should be removable every year and not re-eligible till after a year's interval.[1] It is clear, however, from an examination of the names of the aldermen for the period 1319-76,[2] that this rule was entirely disregarded. For example, at the time of the change, the alderman of Dowgate[3] had held his office since 1352, while two of the aldermen deprived of their charge in 1376, because of their impeachment, had held theirs since 1349.[4] In cases where an election had been very recent it had almost always followed on a long term of office often terminated only by

[1] *Lib. Cust.* 1, p. 269.
[2] To be found in A. B. Beaven's *Aldermen of the City of London*, 1.
[3] *Ibid.* p. 136.   [4] *Ibid.* pp. 167 and 276.

the death of the former alderman.[1] The alderman for Billingsgate [2] had not been changed since 1358, that for Farringdon [3] since 1357. Two aldermen had held office for nine,[4] one for eight [5] and one for seven [6] years. It was therefore a very real change that the king was inaugurating when, on 2 November 1376, he ordered "that every elective [7] alderman of the City in every year . . . shall be entirely removed from the office of his aldermanry, and shall in no wise be re-elected in the following year," "in as much as divers controversies and opinions have arisen between the aldermen and the commonalty over the removal of the aldermen "[8]—the aldermen giving a "sinister interpretation" to the words "sint amobiles per communitatem," declaring that they were only removable on account of misbehaviour, while the commonalty reject this interpretation.[9]

The importance at this time of the office over which the commonalty were attempting to secure more control is, of course, well known. Besides his presidency of the wardmote, which met to enquire into breaches of the peace and of regulations as to residence, into precautions against fire, cleanliness of the streets and other kindred matters, it was the alderman's duty to enforce these regulations, and through him alone could defects be presented to the mayor in the Mayor's Court,[10] in order that they might be remedied.

---

[1] E.g. John de Stodeye had been alderman of Vintry from 1352 to his death in 1376 (*Aldermen of the City of London.* 1, p. 205).

[2] *Ibid.* 1, p. 22.　　　　　　　　　　[3] *Ibid.* 1, p. 142.

[4] *Ibid.* 1, pp. 33 and 188. (Both these men had been aldermen before—in different wards from those they represented in 1376—one from 1356 and the other from 1365. *Ibid.* 1, p. 88.)

[5] *Ibid.* 1, p. 55.　　　　　　　　　　[6] *Ibid.* 1, p. 88.

[7] The alderman of Port-Soken was not elective, but always the Prior of Holy Trinity.　　　　　　[8] *Cal. P.R.* 1374–77, p. 387.

[9] Only six gilds were represented on the Court of Aldermen at the time of the change. There were nine grocers or pepperers, four fishmongers, one vintner, four mercers, two goldsmiths and two drapers; the twenty-third elective member was a lawyer, William Halden, the City Recorder.

[10] *Liber Albus*, 1, pp. 36–8 and 257–60. The *Liber Albus* was compiled in 1419, but as the writer remarks on the recent changes and gives the time when they have occurred—for example he speaks (1, p. 36) of the question of the yearly election of aldermen—it may be inferred that when he speaks of customs, as here, and in other places, without such comment, that these customs had been in force for a considerable time.

It was in his power to punish those officers who worked under his orders, whom the ward-mote had appointed ;[1] he had the power to arrest in the absence of sheriff or bailiff, while if they were present they arrested on his orders ; [2] respect for his authority was strengthened by the penalty of the loss of a hand incurred by anyone who insulted him.[3]

Though he did not deliver judgment in the Court of Husting[4] he was formally summoned to attend,[5] the presence of six aldermen at least being necessary for the legal pronouncement of judgment,[6] as was the presence of at least one in the Sheriff's Court for the same purpose.[7] Judicial functions, moreover, he exercised fully in the " Pie Powder " Courts held by the mayor, sheriffs and aldermen for the purpose of summary jurisdiction in commercial matters[8] and in the Court of the Mayor and Aldermen held in the Outer Chamber of the Guildhall. This court, commonly known as the Mayor's Court, dealt . . . with actions arising out of the common law such as debt, detinue and covenant to any amount, slander, malicious prosecution and assault, as well as with matters coming within the special City customs, including apprenticeship, orphanage, trading by women and offences against the City ordinances.[9] In the same court,[10] when held in the Inner Chamber of the Guildhall, the ordinary administrative business of the City was carried on—ordinances of the misteries, for instance, were approved, and permission granted to orphans in the City's custody to marry [11]—while here were first discussed questions of general policy arising

[1] *Liber Albus*, I, p. 39.   [2] *Ibid.* I, p. 277.

[3] *Ibid.* I, p. 35.

[4] For the jurisdiction of the Court of Husting, see R. R. Sharpe's *Calendar of Wills*, I, Introd. pp. ii–xxxi ; for that of the Sheriff's Court see *Liber Albus*, I, pp. 42, 199, 213–19, and for both, and for that of the Mayor's Court, see A. H. Thomas, *Introd. to Calendar of Early Mayor's Court Rolls.*

[5] *Liber Albus*, I, p. 190.

[6] *Ibid.* I, p. 403.   [7] *Ibid.* I, p. 404.

[8] *Liber Albus*, I, pp. 67 and 390.

[9] Dr. A. H. Thomas in *Trans. Royal Hist. Soc.*, 4th series, IV, p. 85.

[10] Technically there were two distinct courts, but their membership was identical. See A. Pulling, *Laws and Customs of the City*, pp. 31–6 and 177–200.

[11] It was in this court, too, that freedoms were granted and elections ratified, and orders made for the expenditure of City funds.

from demands made by the king or some great noble, or concerning some danger to the City or change needed in its internal organisation—questions for whose final decision the mayor would summon the Common Council,[1] in order that the act might be that of the whole commonalty, though in practice in the fourteenth century it would appear that the opinion of the common councillors seldom had much weight against that of the mayor and aldermen.

It was to an office of such importance, then, that the freemen of each ward elected annually, from 1376–77 to 1393–94, one of their fellow-citizens. By a "precept" issued by the mayor[2] in 1384,[3] confirmed the same year by Parliament,[4] the rule forbidding re-election till after a year's interval was abolished, however; it is, therefore, possible to determine with some certainty how far the abolition of annual elections in 1394 was the desire of the City as a whole, by comparing the membership of the Court of Aldermen at that date with that for the ten years before, and by an analysis of the personnel of the court for the whole period 1377–94. Such an analysis and comparison shows plainly that the power possessed by the wards of electing a different alderman each year had not resulted in widening to any noticeable extent the circle from which the aldermen were drawn. The last annual election may serve for example. Three only of the aldermen of 1393 failed to secure re-election, while only one of the twenty-three elected in 1394 had never served as an alderman before.[5] During the first seven years of annual elections, when re-election could not take place until after the interval of a year, the lists of aldermen certainly do show a desire on the part of the wards to elect new men; having regard, however, to the wording of the king's Letter Patent on the subject,[6] it is significant that the number of those from whom the wards elect is so small. As the number of wards, exclusive of Portsoken,[7] was at this time twenty-three, the least

---

[1] Or some less formal "congregatio." See below, p. 36.
[2] Nicholas Brembre.
[3] In February, the month of Northampton's arrest (*Cal. L.B.H*, p. 228). The king's confirmation was received in March (*ibid.* p. 231).
[4] *Rot. Parl.* III, pp. 172–3.
[5] Beaven, *Aldermen*, I, pp. 402–3.
[6] Quoted above, p. 31.
[7] See above, p. 31, n. 7.

number of men that could have held office was forty-six, the greatest a hundred and sixty-one ; the actual number which did so was eighty-six. Of the forty men in excess of the minimum, however, eleven can be accounted for by five deaths[1] and two deprivations[2] occurring among existing aldermen, and by the fact that four more were excluded from office because of their trial for high treason.[3] As it is also probable, from the fact that no further mention of them occurs in the City records, that eight others[4] died during these seven years, the excess over the minimum which could have held office may even be reduced to twenty-one.

Of the twenty-three aldermen in office in 1376, seventeen[5] found re-election between 1377 and 1384, eight of these continuing to serve at a subsequent period.[6] When, in 1384, re-election without interval became possible, the circle grew smaller still. For the next ten years the number of aldermen is fifty-two.[7] Of these thirty-eight had held

---

[1] R. Lucas, J. Pyel, R. Launde, W. Knyghtcote, and R. Hatfield (see Dr. Sharpe's *Calendar of Wills*, II).

[2] Nicholas Exton in August 1382 " for opprobrious words used to John of Northampton, then Mayor ". He lost his citizenship in the following November, but the judgments were reversed in June 1384 (*Cal. L.B.H*, pp. 196, 205 and 233–4), and Adam Karlill, grocer, who was debarred in August 1382 from filling any public office in the City and from wearing a livery " party-furred with fur or lined with silk " on the pain of losing his franchise. He was not an alderman at the time, and was not debarred for his share in the 1381 risings (see below, Chapter IV), but for his conduct towards the " strange fish-mongers while selling their fish at the Stokkes " (*Cal. L.B.H*, p. 197). This judgment was also reversed in 1384. Northampton was accused of trying to exclude John Philpot also, John More charging him with corruption during his mayoralty, in reality because of his opposition to Northampton's election as mayor (*Peasants' Rising and the Lollards*, p. 29), and Walsingham thought he succeeded (*Hist. Ang.* II, p. 71), but the records of his elections as alderman of Cornhill (*L.B.H*, fos. 140 and 174) show that this was not so. Probably Philpot was too popular in the City, where his public spirit in money matters must have been well known (e.g. see below, pp. 47–9). There is, however, a record of a case which he brought against Robert Parys, ironmonger, and his wife for having slanderously accused him of taking a bribe in a lawsuit. It is undated (Files of Actions of Mayor's Court Rolls).

[3] Sibil, Horn, Tonge and Frossh (Réville, pp. 190–9).

[4] A. Lovekyn, W. Betele, J. Morton, J. Brian, A. Stable, H. Begge, R. Aillesbury and J. Maryns. It is possible that Maryns did not die till 1385 (*Cal. Wills*, II, p. 248).

[5] Beaven, I, p. 392.   [6] *Ibid.* pp. 399–403.   [7] *Ibid.*

the office before, while of the fourteen new men, eleven
were necessary to fill the places of ten aldermen who had
died [1] and one who had obtained permission from the
mayor to retire ; [2] this would account for all but three of
the fresh names.

One may suspect John of Northampton as the prime
mover in the change of 1377 ; that he was such seemed to
his enemies a plausible accusation to put forward at his
trial ; [3] this is not proof in itself, however, as he was also
accused, falsely,[4] of ordaining the annual election of aldermen and the election of the Common Council to be by
misteries, during his mayoralty.[5] Apart from the fact,
however, that the change is in line with his general policy
of attacking the capitalists of the City, who, for their part,
abolished the bar to immediate re-election at the same
time as they were procuring his disgrace,[6] it is noteworthy
that only six [7] of his supporters ever held the office of alderman, and that of these six, none had done so before 1377
and only two continued to do so after 1384,[8] one of whom,
Adam Bamme, left Northampton's party on the latter's
failure to secure re-election as mayor in October 1383.

The cessation of annual elections in 1394 did little more
than confirm an already existing state of affairs. The
agitation which procured the letters patent had not
sufficient strength behind it to overcome those forces of
wealth in the few and dislike of the burdens of office in
the many [9] which were probably the main support of the

[1] N. Twyford, R. Warbulton, W. Walworth, N. Brembre, T. Cornwaleys,
J. Eston, T. Carleton, N. Exton, J. Boseham and J. Rote (see Sharpe, *Cal.
of Wills*, II, and MS. Index to Commissary of London Registers).

[2] R. de Preston (Beaven, I, p. 400).

[3] Powell and Trevelyan, *Peasants' Rising and the Lollards*, p. 28.

[4] *Ibid.*

[5] A. Stable was mayor in the former instance, J. Warde in the latter.

[6] *Cal. L.B.H*, p. 240.

[7] More, Norbury, Vyne, A. Bamme, Carleton and Noket. See Beaven, I.

[8] A. Bamme and Carleton.

[9] E.g. John Wrothe, fishmonger, discharged at his request " owing to
press of business abroad " (*Cal. L.B.H*, p. 48, cf. Exton's plea, *ibid.* p. 196),
and an instance in the fifteenth century (*L.B.L*, fos. 586 and 646), cited by
Dr. Thrupp (in her unprinted London thesis on " A Study of the Merchant
Class of London in the 15th C. with special reference to the Coy. of Grocers "),
of a draper imprisoned for evading the duties of an alderman.

monopoly system. The experience of Northampton's mayoralty, however, made it seem worth while to his opponents to revert to the system of infrequent elections, while they further strengthened their monopolistic position by ordaining in 1397 [1] that each ward must nominate two candidates out of which the mayor and aldermen should choose their new colleague. Five years later this number was increased to four. [2]

The second important constitutional change in the City during this period was in the mode of election of the Common Council. This change took place in 1376 [3] and was reversed in 1384 ; [4] since then the principle governing such elections remains unaltered, though there was an unsuccessful effort to alter it in 1389. [5] Professor Tait has shown that the lasting importance of what was done in 1376 lies in the establishment for the first time in London of a representative assembly of workable numbers which had the right to be consulted by the mayor and aldermen at least once a quarter. [6] His analysis of earlier assemblies shows plainly that even if the expression " common council " be used of them for convenience sake, they were not the standing councils with fixed rights and duties which existed after 1376. [7] The expression is used below, therefore, with this caveat.

Although it was only for eight years that the City elected its Common Council through the misteries instead of through the wards the experiment is worth considering in some detail for the light it throws on political and economic conditions in London in the last quarter of the fourteenth century.

First, there are signs that this innovation was violently opposed ; unanimity on the question was only reached by the City under threat of interference by the king ; [8] when, in 1384, a return was made to election by wards, the reason

[1] *Cal. L.B.H*, p. 436.   [2] *Cal. L.B.I*, p. 18.
[3] *Cal. L.B.H*, pp. 39–40.   [4] *Ibid.* p. 240.
[5] *Ibid.* pp. 279–80.
[6] J. Tait, *The Mediaeval English Borough*, pp. 313–14. He emphasises how exceptional London was in this respect (*ibid.* p. 316).
[7] *The Mediaeval English Borough*, pp. 304–11.
[8] *Cal. L.B.H*, pp. 35–6.

given for the change was that disturbances had continually
arisen because the method of election resulted in unsuitable
persons obtaining seats, and in decisions being come to
" by shouting rather than by sense."[1]

Was John of Northampton, the reputed author of so
much discord, the originator of this short-lived and much
opposed method of election ?[2] It is almost certain that he
was, at any rate, its chief promoter. He was accused of
being so at his trial,[3] and we have evidence in the City
records which supports the accusation. The change of 1376
was carried out, in accordance with powers conferred on them
by charter[4] thirty-five years before, by the mayor, aldermen
and commonalty of the City—the " Commonalty " consisting in this case of an assembly itself elected by the
misteries and not by the wards. This assembly had been
summoned by the mayor to discuss and settle certain
specified matters, of which this question of the mode of
election was one ; he had taken this step with the advice
of five aldermen and eight commoners ; Northampton and
Nicholas Twyford[5] together with two mercers[6] and another
goldsmith,[7] were the aldermen ; of the eight commoners,
five were later Northampton's most noted supporters.[8]
Further, Brembre, Philpot and Walworth, the heads of the
party opposed to Northampton, were not among those who
advised the mayor to act in this way, nor did they attend
the assembly summoned on this advice which passed the
ordinances giving the power of election to the gilds.[9]
Walworth, in his mayoralty, made an effort to change the

---

[1] *Liber Albus,* I, p. 461.

[2] It was not altogether a novelty, representation by misteries having been
tried in 1312 and again after 1351, though the motive seems to have been
entirely different. Tait, *op. cit.* p. 309.

[3] *Peasants' Rising and the Lollards,* p. 28.

[4] That of 15 E III (*Lib. Cust.* II, pp. 443–4) which had granted to the
mayor and aldermen the power of amending defective or obsolete customs,
with the consent of the commonalty.

[5] Twyford seems later to have changed his opinions on the matter. See
Cal. L.B.H, p. 347, and below, p. 38, n. 3.

[6] Adam Stable and John Fifhide.

[7] J. Chichestre.

[8] Norbury, More, Essex, Fraunceys and Willarby. *Cal. L.B.H,* p. 38.

[9] *Cal. L.B.H,* p. 40. See above, Chapter II, p. 18.

system,[1] while Brembre in the first year of his second term of office succeeded in doing so.[2]

On the face of things, therefore, the episode seems to be an effort, successful for eight years, to transfer the control of the membership of the Common Council from the wards to the gilds—an effort only frustrated by the ruin of the whole party which supported it, at the time of Northampton's imprisonment. This explanation, however, though it is certainly the most obvious one, does not account for the fact that there is so little trace of any further dispute on the subject,[3] more important, it leaves unexplained what the transference of power from the wards to the gilds really meant. It might be assumed that to Northampton it was a means of checking the victualling gilds or of increasing the power of the smaller gilds ;[4] the similarity of circumstance and coincidence of date point to some connection with the attack on the monopoly of the office of alderman. Investigation of the composition of those Common Councils whose membership is recorded, however, qualifies this view by one outstanding fact. If such were indeed Northampton's aims, he did not attain them by securing that election of common councillors should be through the gilds, for the proportion between the gild representatives remains roughly the same, and so to a large extent does the personnel, however the councils are elected and however they vote. Unfortunately no list of councillors exists for the period 1351–76, either in the Letter Books

---

[1] *Cal. L.B.H*, p. 156. Prof. Tait considers he was successful (*op. cit.* p. 313). As there are no lists of councillors for this year it is impossible to prove whether he was or not.

[2] *Ibid.* p. 240.

[3] In 1389, when Nicholas Twyford, goldsmith, was mayor, it was agreed that because of controversy as to the mode of election, the Common Councils in future should be chosen by the mayor, in the presence of at least twelve aldermen, from each ward, without paying regard to their mistery (*Cal. L.B.H*, p. 347). Dr. Sharpe thinks it improbable this came into force (*ibid.* Introd. p. viii). It is difficult to judge, as there are no lists of councillors between 1388 and 1458–59 (*Cal. L.B.K*, p. 179).

[4] See Unwin, *Gilds and Companies*, pp. 131–2. Dr. Stubbs (*Const. Hist.* II, p. 575) thought that the change shut out the lower classes from the Council, a view to some extent borne out by analysis of its members (see below, pp. 40–1).

or in the Plea and Memoranda Rolls,[1] so that it is impossible
to determine what change in membership was caused by
the adoption of election by gilds in 1376. It may, however,
be conjectured that, judging by later events, whatever
change there may have been, it was not a great one.

For the period 1376–84 we possess lists of members of
three Common Councils elected by the gilds—those of
1376,[2] 1377[3] and 1381[4]—a council elected by fifty-one
misteries in 1377 is mentioned[5] as are three councils elected
partly from the misteries and partly from the wards,[6] and
one in 1381[7] consisting of ex-aldermen " together with the
more powerful cominers from the several wards."

In January 1383–84 was passed the ordinance fixing the
number of common councillors at ninety-six, to be elected
by the wards in proportion to their size, with the proviso
that the mayor was not to accept more than eight of one
gild.[8] This ordinance was confirmed in 1385;[9] it may
have been modified in 1388–89[10] but the gilds, at anyrate,
did not secure any right of election.[11] Of Common Council
so elected there are membership lists for nine—those of
June,[12] August[13] and October[14] 1384, of March[15] 1384–85,
of March 1385–86[16] and August 1388,[17] together with three

---

[1] The names of the members of an assembly or council which met probably
in 1285 are recorded (*Cal. L.B.A*, pp. 209–10). They are 50 in number,
10 of them having been crossed out. The next list of names is in 1351 (*Cal.
L.B.F*, pp. 238–9) there are 54 of them.

[2] *Cal. L.B.H*, pp. 42–4.   [3] *Ibid.* p. 59.

[4] *Cal. P. and M.R.* 1381–1412, pp. 29–31.

[5] *Cal. L.B.H*, p. 64.

[6] In 1379 and 1380, *ibid.* pp. 137, 155.

[7] *Ibid.* p. 164.   [8] *Ibid.* pp. 227–8.

[9] *Ibid.* p. 277.

[10] *Ibid.* p. 347. But see above, p. 38.

[11] Norton asserts (Commentaries 116) that the gilds retained the right
of election of mayor and sheriffs, but the ordinances of 1384 (*Ibid.*,
p. 241) declare the election to lie with the Common Council and " others
of more sufficient men of the City " whom the mayor and aldermen should
summon. No mention is made of the gilds.

[12] *Cal. P. and M.R.* 1381–1412, pp. 53–4.

[13] *Cal. L.B.H*, pp. 237–40.

[14] *Cal. P. and M.R.* 1381–1412, pp. 84–9.

[15] *Ibid.* 1381–1412, pp. 54–5.

[16] *Cal. L.B.H*, pp. 279–81.   [17] *Ibid.* pp. 332–4.

dated less precisely—one Anno 8 Ric. II,[1] another 1386[2] and a third of the time of Nicholas Exton, mayor, 1386-87.[3]

In the Letter Book H, when the election is by wards, the names, but not the gilds, of the members are given, and this is often the case in the Plea and Memoranda Rolls. It is possible, however, because these Rolls do sometimes give the gilds, and through further mention of the men in question in the Letter Books, the Plea and Memoranda Rolls and the Husting Rolls, to discover the gilds of the great majority of the members of all these councils. This is rendered easier by the fact that to a considerable extent the same men year after year were returned, either by the same ward, or, in a few cases, by a different one.

As a result of this classification[4] it is possible to draw certain definite conclusions. First, all through the period, however the Common Council is elected and whatever line of policy it pursues, there is always a marked majority of members drawn from the non-victualling gilds as well as a majority of those gilds over the victualling gilds.[5] This is true even of assemblies such as those of the 31 August 1384 and of March 1384-85 which were not Common Councils in the strict sense of the term, and whose members were probably selected by the mayor and aldermen. Secondly, there are a certain number of occupations which only receive representation on the Council when the election is made by the wards—pulters, hostillers, malt-mongers, pie-bakers, bladers,[6] woolmongers, corders, fynours, bell-makers, furnagers, coopers, shethers, corsours, jewellers, potters, fruiters, barbers, carters, paternostrers, chaloners,[7] and glovers. On the other hand the leathersellers, bowyers, loriners, horners, spurriers, pinners, fustours, and white-

---

[1] *Cal. P. and M.R.* 1381-1412, pp. 91-2.
[2] *Ibid.* pp. 122-4.   [3] *Ibid.* pp. 132-3.
[4] See Appendix II for details illustrating this chapter. In cases when the lists are of assemblies rather than of Common Councils the common councillors form a good proportion of the members.
[5] The lists that exist do not, therefore, bear out Mr. E. F. Meyer's conjecture that the victualling gilds " by use of the ward system might obtain continuous control of the council " (*Speculum* VII, p. 250).
[6] I.e. corn merchants.
[7] Makers of blanket cloth.

tawyers, and perhaps the cappers,[1] are only represented when election is by misteries. It would seem therefore that the second method of election was no more democratic than the first, perhaps slightly less so, though the reverse opinion has sometimes been held.[2] The lists of members also show that the rule laid down in 1384 that the mayor should not accept more than eight members of any mistery, even if more were elected, was not strictly kept, and that the regulation that there should be ninety-six members was also sometimes disregarded.

The first conclusion is, of course, the most important one. It points to one of two things—either there was no such cleavage on policy and personalities, as is generally supposed, between the victualling and non-victualling gilds of the City at this time, or else the independent power of the Common Council towards the end of the fourteenth century was very slight, and the councillors were careful to express only such opinions as they thought would please the mayor and aldermen for the time being. Against the first explanation there is abundant evidence, in the Rolls of Parliament and all through the Letter Books G and H and the Plea and Memoranda Rolls for the period, of innumerable affrays, riots and disputes arising from the jealousy between victuallers and non-victuallers ; in favour of the alternative, it is recorded that the assembly which petitioned the king for Northampton's execution in March 1384–85 contained one of his known supporters[3] as did that which resolved the following year that he should not be allowed within 100 miles of the City ;[4] there were two[5] in that of June 1384 which declared all the disturbances since Brembre's election the fault of Northampton ; while

[1] " Hatters " are found in ward lists, " Cappers " in those chosen by the misteries.

[2] Of the twenty-one occupations unrepresented by election by misteries only six are those of victuallers.

[3] Geoffrey Waldern, draper. The non-victualling majority at this Council was 34.

[4] This was Thomas Noket, draper ; this assembly had a non-victualling majority of between 27 and 47.

[5] J. Doncaster, copper-smith, and Geoff. Waldern—the non-victualling majority being 23.

in August of the same year was held a council or assembly which agreed to pray the king to punish Northampton, of which it is expressly said that no one said a word to the contrary, though invited to do so fearlessly ; at this assembly the non-victualling majority was between fifty-two and ninety-four, of whom four [1] of those mentioned at Northampton's trial as his followers were members. The invitation to speak out fearlessly, followed by complete silence, might even be held to have a somewhat sinister interpretation when it is considered that the party of small masters of the non-victualling misteries which Northampton undoubtedly represented, was so much in the majority.[2] It was no doubt the aim of the aldermen to have as little interference as possible with their actions on the part of the Common Council, and this aim was favoured by Common Councils elected by wards, in which craft feeling, as opposed to deference to the opinion of the alderman of the ward, would not have such free play as in a council directly representative of the misteries.[3] It does not seem, however, that much opposition was ever offered by the councillors to the party in power, in whatever way they were elected.

The third change made in 1376 related to the election of the mayor and one of the sheriffs.[4] By the same ordinance [5] which gave the election of common councillors into the hands of the misteries it was decreed that only common councillors elected in this manner should come to the elections of mayor and sheriffs, whereas heretofore only those who were specially summoned could attend such elections—the power

---

[1] J. Carbonell, goldsmith, J. Longe, Thomas Lincolle, draper, and Geoff. Waldern.

[2] In the petitions of the crafts against Brembre in 1386 he is accused of using armed force at election time and of making " dyverse enarmynges bi day and eke bi nyght " but not specifically of threatening the common council by force, except during elections. See below, Chapter VI, p. 94.

[3] This statement must be modified by the fact that in some cases wards and misteries were very closely connected. Vintry Ward, for example, is represented by the same four vintners in each of the six councils elected by wards of which there are lists in the *P. and M.R.*; but this is an exceptional case. Even Bridge Ward, where the Fishmongers were strong, never had only Fishmongers as representatives.

[4] The other was nominated by the mayor for the time being.

[5] *Cal. L.B.H*, p. 39.

of summons resting with the mayor and aldermen,[1] who had
to choose men from each ward in proportion to its size.[2]

In 1384, at the same time that the election of common
councillors was given back to the wards, it was ordained [3]
that for the election of mayor and sheriff, the mayor for the
time being, with the advice of sixteen aldermen at least,
should summon not only the Common Council, but " others
of the more sufficient men of the City, to make the said
election, so many and such as seem to them necessary for
the time." [4] In the case of an election to the mayoralty,
two men were to be elected of whom the mayor and aldermen should choose one. A year later the circle of candidates
for the office of mayor was limited by an ordinance declaring
no one could be mayor except an ex-sheriff.[5] These ordinances remained in force till 1475.[6]

It is obvious that this method gave a preponderant
influence in elections to the existing office-holders of the
City, and was logically in keeping with the rest of the monopoly system of government, described earlier in this chapter,
which was established by the end of the fourteenth century
—established only the more rigidly because of the attempt
to overthrow it by that section of the citizens which is
known as the party of Northampton.

[1] *Cal. L.B.G*, p. 265.

[2] *Cal. L.B.F*, p. 304. In practice it was probably the same men who were
summoned as those who would have been called to represent the commonalty
on any other occasion.

[3] *Cal. L.B.H*, pp. 241–2.

[4] That which re-elected Brembre as mayor in October 1384, for example,
contained 231 ordinary citizens as well as 93 common councillors (*Cal.
P. and M.R.* 1381–1412, pp. 84–9). Compare the addition to the common
councillors of some of " the more reputable and substantial men of the
(wards) in such numbers that the Council had to remove from the upper
chamber of the Guildhall to the hall below "—when the " Jubile Book "
was condemned to be burnt in 1387 (*Memorials*, p. 494).

[5] *Cal. L.B.H*, p. 277.

[6] *Cal. L.B.L*, p. 132 (except for a slight change in 1467), *ibid.* p. 73.
Norton in his commentaries (pp. 116 and 126–7) misinterpreted the ordinances,
and his error is repeated by Stubbs (*Const. Hist.* III, p. 875). This has been
pointed out by Dr. Sharpe (*Cal. L.B.H*, VIII, n. 1.) and (in the most recent
discussion of the question) by Prof. Tait (*Med. Eng. Borough*, pp. 314 and 315).
Professor Tait also points out that " London stood alone in the development
of a separate electoral assembly " (*ibid.* p. 316).

CHAPTER IV

THE EARLY YEARS OF RICHARD II, AND THE RISINGS OF 1381 AS THEY AFFECTED LONDON

THE reign of Edward III closed with London united by the fear and anger aroused by John of Gaunt's threat to its liberties and independence—the threat, that is, of a man who appeared at that moment to be able to persuade the king to anything he wished.[1] The coming of the new king gave the Londoners their chance, and they took it.[2] The events of the next four years suggest very strongly indeed that London was making a considerable, and, at times, a not unsuccessful effort at least to share in the central government, if not actually to control it. By " London " must be understood the group of capitalists already described, who, in spite of the recent constitutional changes in the City, succeeded in keeping the office of mayor for one of their number till October 1381 ;[3] their chief opponent during these four years was John of Gaunt, supported at times by his brother, Thomas of Woodstock, and strengthened by the irritation felt by the majority of the great landowners at the interference of the merchants in a province

[1] Only a month before Edward died the mayor and aldermen had had to appear before the King's Council to give their reasons against the Bill for extending the Marshal's jurisdiction ; these reasons when given were not accepted as sufficient (*Cal. L.B.H*, p. 57).

[2] Note their petition for assurance of the privilege that only their own officers should arrest in the City (*Rot. Parl.* III, p. 28), presented in Richard's first Parliament ; it met with a favourable reply.

[3] Brembre was mayor from March 1376–77 to October 1378, Philpot from October 1378 to October 1379, Hadley from October 1379 to October 1380 and Walworth from October 1380 to October 1381, when John de Northampton was elected and remained in office till October 1383. For Hadley's later relationship by marriage to Brembre and Philpot, see Appendix I.

they considered their own.[1] It is probably from this period that dates the hatred of the future "Lords Appellant," and particularly of the future Duke of Gloucester,[2] for Nicholas Brembre, a hatred which helped to cost the latter his life in 1388.

As soon as Edward's death was certain, and even before it had actually taken place, Philpot and other Londoners had an interview with the future Richard II and those whom his father had placed round him, who were to form the backbone of his council in the early years of his reign. The citizens declared their intention of supporting the future Government, and stated their case against Lancaster.[3]

A short time after Richard's accession a formal reconciliation took place in his presence,[4] and although in the Parliament of October 1377 the petition of the Londoners for the right to exercise jurisdiction in Southwark over those who had escaped there from the City officers was again refused,[5] the Government promised to order the lords of the franchises concerned to punish the offenders themselves.[6] In the same Parliament the constable and marshal petitioned against the interference of the mayor and sheriffs of London when they were attempting " a faire . . . execucion sur ceux qe sount enfraunchisez en vostre dit Cite," [7] but they petitioned to no purpose, and the whole matter was apparently dropped. It would have been difficult to have pursued it further in face of the opposition of men on whom so much depended at this moment. A council was called in August [8] to discuss the question of defence of the coast and of shipping—the French, mean-

---

[1] This irritation is brought out very clearly by the writer of the *Chronicon Angliae*, particularly when he is describing Philpot's expedition against the pirate (*Chron. Ang.* pp. 199, 200).

[2] See below, p. 48, for the reason for this.

[3] *Chron. Ang.* pp. 146–7 ; *Hist. Anglic.* I, p. 329.

[4] " Et in signum non fictae pacis, osculatus est ibidem omnes et singulos coram rege " (*Chron. Ang.* pp. 148–9).

[5] It is probable that those who broke the monopoly of the fishmongers are particularly meant when " vitaillers " are mentioned.

[6] *Rot. Parl.* III, p. 19. Henry IV granted the mayor and commonalty of London the long desired power to arrest felons and malefactors in Southwark in 1406 (*Lib. Cust.* p. 433).

[7] *Rot. Parl.* III, p. 30.   [8] *Cal. L.B.H*, p. 73.

while, illustrating the urgency of the question by capturing the Isle of Wight and burning the Sussex coast towns.[1] The London members of this council were Walworth, Philpot, Karlille and Hadley.[2] If Chaucer had not been even more discreet where politics were concerned than were the writers of the City records themselves, any of these men—or Nicholas Brembre equally well—might have supplied him with a name for his nameless merchant, for, as passionately as he, they " wolde the see were kept for any thing "—though by no means only " bitwixe Middelburgh and Orewelle." [3] The next few months were to show how much they were prepared to do in this cause. In the following month the four London members of the council raised the sum of £10,000 as a loan to the Government, becoming attorneys for the other parties to the loan,[4] while in October the City itself advanced £5000.[5] Parliament met in the same month, the City members being Karlille, Walter Sibil, fishmonger, Walworth and Philpot ; [6] the two last being appointed " Treasurers " of the grant made by Parliament, to ensure that it should all be spent on the French war.[7] Peter de la Mare's speech in this Parliament, which contained a defence of the merchants' point of view, shows which way public opinion was tending in face of the danger from the French.[8] The immediate

[1] *Chron. Ang.* pp. 151 and 166–70.

[2] Both Karlille and Hadley were grocers.

[3] Prologue to the *Canterbury Tales*, lines 276–7. They must, of course, all have been known to Chaucer (Kirk, *Life Records of Chaucer, passim*).

[4] *Cal. P.R.* 1377–81, p. 24. The other creditors are not named, but in the roll itself they are described as " autres certeins merchantz si bien de nostre Roialme dengleterre come autres . . . et les ditz merchantz qe la dit somme nous ount ensi cheviz ount fait les avant ditz Nicholas William Johan et Johan lour attournes pur seurte ent prendre sufficiantement de nous." Nicholas must be a slip as the fourth man's name was John.

[5] *Cal. L.B.H*, p. 79. Compare the £1000 voted by the citizens during 1371 " to safeguard their ships at sea " (*Cal. L.B.G*, p. 282). (I am indebted for this reference to Mr. Mead.)

[6] *Cal. L.B.H*, p. 75.

[7] *Rot. Parl.* III, p. 7. (The appointment of Treasurers was the condition on which the grant was made.)

[8] E.g. " Quant les Marchantz du Roialme furent Seigneurs et Maistres, et avoient la disposition et ordinance de lours propres Niefs, si estoit la Navye du Roialme grande et pleintinouse " (*Rot. Parl.* III, p. 5).

reward for the financial services of the Londoners was the confirmation in the same Parliament of the City's privilege " qe nul Estrange de la Franchise . . . vende ou achate d'autre Estrange aucunes Marchandises," [1] while on 4 December a very full " Inspeximus " Charter was accorded to the City. [2] The loan itself was repaid in the following March, out of the king's customs at the Port of London— the customers at that time being Philpot and Brembre. [3]

· Meanwhile, efforts were being made against the French. John of Gaunt led an expedition into Brittany, [4] and several sea engagements were fought ; [5] the piracy in the Channel, however, continued to flourish, so that Philpot, despairing of anything being effected by the royal ships, fitted out a fleet of his own, and achieved a great triumph by the capture of John Mercer, a Scottish pirate in alliance with the French, who had lately made a very destructive raid upon English ships in the neighbourhood of Cherbourg. [6]

The contrast between this exploit and the ill-success of the Brittany expedition was not calculated to modify the duke's ill-will towards Philpot and his friends. His attack on them was made in October 1378. The Parliament of that date was held at Gloucester instead of at Westminster, at the instigation of John of Gaunt, [7] for fear of resistance from the Bishops [8] and the Londoners ; the duke succeeded in removing Walworth and Philpot from their position as " Treasurers," [9] though it was acknowledged that the

---

[1] *Rot. Parl.* III, p. 27.

[2] Birch, *Hist. Charters*, p. 69 ; Maitland, pp. 143–4. Special mention is made in the charter not only of the monopoly of trade spoken of above, but of the right of changing customs in the City by the mayor, aldermen and commonalty.

[3] *Cal. L.B.H*, p. 88. The £10,000 advanced by the merchants was repaid May 1378 (*Cal. P.R.* 1377–81, p. 219).

[4] *Chron. Ang.* pp. 204–6 ; *Hist. Anglic.* I, p. 373.

[5] *Ibid.* pp. 343–4, 364–5, 368. *Chron. Ang.* p. 170 (attack on the English fisheries), pp. 171–3, 191–7. (The chronicler inveighs very much against the slackness of John of Gaunt and the other nobles.)

[6] *Hist. Anglic.* I, pp. 370–1 ; *Chron. Ang.* pp. 199–200.

[7] *Ibid.* p. 211.

[8] An attack was about to be made on the privileges of sanctuary and the question of confiscating Church property was discussed.

[9] *Chron. Ang.* p. 194.

account they submitted proved that the entire grant had been spent on the war ; [1] further, the monopoly of the victualling trades in London was abolished by a statute [2] which allowed free trade in corn, flesh, fish and all kinds of other foodstuffs and also all kinds of spices, of fruit, of fur and of small or little " merceries " such as silk, gold and silver thread, head coverings and other such little " merceries," though wine was still to be sold by strangers by wholesale only, as were " All the other great ' merceries ' as cloths of gold and silver, of silk, of thin silk, of heavy linen, of linen such as canvas and of other such great ' merceries '."[3] It is arguable that it was by his support of this measure that John of Northampton,[4] one of the City members of this Parliament,[5] was brought to the duke's notice as a possible ally in London.[6] Thomas of Woodstock, then Earl of Buckingham, for his part, made a violent attack on Brembre. During his mayoralty a certain John Maynard " wex-chaundler " and " other misdoers of his covin " had assaulted the earl's servants upon Cornhill, had pursued them to the earl's hostel and broken the door down, " the said earl being then within and lying in his bed and by reason thereof no little alarmed." [7] The earl accused Brembre of negligence over this incident and succeeded in convincing him that it was worth while appeasing him by a gift of 100 marks.[8] This, however, was

[1] *Rot. Parl.* III, pp. 35-6 ; *Cal. P.R.* 1377-81, p. 327.

[2] Statutes of the Realm 2 R. II, St. I. c. i.

[3] It is noticeable that the fishmongers were the hardest hit of the important victualling gilds by this statute—the vintners would not suffer at all, and the grocers little in comparison, because they dealt in such a variety of goods. See Dr. Thrupp's article on the " Grocers of London " in *English Trade in the 15th Century* (Power and Postan) and particularly her statement that " both grocers and drapers sold canvas, linen and thread " (*ibid.* p. 282).

[4] There is no record of his having supported it, but in view of his campaign of attack on the victuallers three years later and of the fact that the statute protects his own mistery—that of the drapers—it is very unlikely he did not do so.   [5] *Cal. L.B.H*, p. 98.

[6] Dr. Sharpe (*ibid.* n. 1) assumes that Northampton was at this time a staunch supporter of the duke and a follower of Wiclif, but brings forward no evidence to support either claim.

[7] *Memorials*, pp. 424 and 427.

[8] *Cal. L.B.H*, p. 111. Brembre was regarded as something of a hero when he returned home, and was indemnified by his fellow-citizens, because

not the only bribe that was necessary, for we find that in the following January a loan of nearly £600 was raised among the citizens of London (to be repaid from the City purse within the next two years) in order to persuade the " great lords of the realm "[1] to return to London, whence they had withdrawn themselves, " to the great damage of the City and specially to victuallers and hostellers," because of the accusations against the Londoners made in the Parliament at Gloucester.[2]

In spite of all this, however, the merchants continued to support the Government in the hope of effecting something against France. In October 1378 Philpot and Brembre joined with Sir Hugh Calverley in binding themselves to pay £2166 13s. 4d. " in service of the war " to William van de Voorde of Bruges;[3] in the following March Philpot and Walworth lent the Government £100,[4] while the City at the same date advanced £5000;[5] in September 1379, Philpot, Launde and St. Ives, together with Sir Robert Knolles, lent £566 13s. 4d.,[6] while in the September of 1380 the City lent £2000;[7] further, the expedition which took place in this year was financed by Philpot and Sir Robert Knolles.[8] The year before, two London fishmongers, Walter Sibil and John Horn, had been concerned in the financial organisation of a small fleet set up to protect the North Sea and its coasts.[9] That this support must have involved at least an attempt at control of policy seems certain, but the only direct evidence there is of such an attempt is that Walworth and Philpot were both members of the commission to investigate and remedy the methods of government expenditure, set up by the Parliament of

---

Walworth and the four City members (including Northampton) declared he had borne himself well in the encounter with the earl, and had paid the 100 marks for fear a statute should be made which should infringe the liberties of the City (see *Memorials*, pp. 424 and 427).

[1] John of Gaunt's accounts and registers give some idea of the great value of his custom to the London victuallers.

[2] *Cal. L.B.H*, pp. 123–4. [3] *Cal. P.R.* 1377–81, p. 280.
[4] *Ibid*. p. 328. [5] *Ibid*. p. 340.
[6] *Ibid*. pp. 385–6. [7] *Ibid*. p. 461.
[8] *Ibid*. 1381–85, p. 361. (See also *Chron. Ang.* p. 266.)
[9] *Rot. Parl.* III, p. 63.

January 1379–80,[1] which secured the appointment of the
Earl of Warwick as the king's governor, and the dismissal
of the chancellor appointed by John of Gaunt at Gloucester.
In the autumn, however, Parliament was held at Northampton instead of at Westminster against the will of the
Londoners,[2] " by the will of the Duke of Lancaster . . . for
truly he considered the ancient hatred yet persisting between himself and the Londoners." It was at this Parliament
that there took place the trial and execution of John
Kirkeby,[3] the Londoner who had, the year before, murdered
a Genoese merchant who was at that time proposing to the
Government to make of Southampton such a port as should
have no equal in the whole of west Europe. The Londoners
were, of course, furious at the suggestion, particularly as
the Genoese was not being received unfavourably, and the
chronicler gives the expectation that they would not have
permitted his execution if Parliament had been held near
London, another reason, besides the wishes of John of
Gaunt, for holding it far away.[4]

Behind the encouragement given to the Genoese by
the Government, may there not have been a feeling that
it would be as well to create some counterpoise to London?
Do the facts that the Government borrowed nothing from
the City or from any Londoner between September 1380
and September 1382, while there is a record of £4000 lent
by a Lombard in May 1381,[5] £2500 by the same man in
the following February [6] and £2800 in August 1382 [7] support
the view that there was such a desire? The absence of a

---

[1] *Rot. Parl.* III, pp. 72–4. (There were 3 bishops, 3 earls, 3 bannerets, 3
knights and 3 merchants, the third being Thomas Graa of York.)

[2] *Chron. Ang.* p. 280. Walsingham softens the phrase " nutu ducis Lan-
castriae " to " nutu quorundam consiliariorum " and puts the " consideravit "
into the plural (*Hist. Anglic.* I, p. 449), cf. the story of the treason of Ralph
Ferrers discovered by Philpot, where Ferrers is said to have been saved from
punishment by the duke in the *Chron. Ang.* account (pp. 278–9), while
Walsingham only hints at who it was from whom he received encouragement
(*Hist. Anglic.* I, pp. 447–8).   [3] Probably a draper.

[4] *Chron. Ang.* pp. 237–9 and 280–1, and *Rot. Parl.* III, p. 75. This Parliament granted the poll-tax, and one of its London members was William Tonge,
vintner, later one of the " rebels of 1381 " (Beaven, I, p. 268).

[5] *Cal. P.R.* 1381–85, p. 4.   [6] *Ibid.* p. 102.
[7] *Ibid.* p. 154.

City loan may, it is true, be accounted for by the length of time which the king was taking to repay the money advanced in September 1380.[1] However that may be, it is certain that the temporary cessation of the City's financial support of the king does not coincide with the change in the balance of power in the City itself which was involved in the election of John of Northampton as mayor in October 1381. This change, however, possibly lengthened the period in which the king obtained no money from London.

The loan in September 1382, of £1333 6s. 8d. was from Brembre ;[2] the City itself did not advance anything till 22 September 1383, just three weeks before Brembre replaced Northampton as mayor ;[3] an attempt had been made in May 1382 to raise a sum among the merchants to finance Richard's proposed expedition to France ; the merchants chosen by the lords to discuss the question were fourteen in number, seven of whom, Philpot, Brembre, Hadley, Fastolf,[4] Organ,[5] William More [6] and Venour,[7] were Londoners ; the answer they returned is significant— " And the merchants hesitate to make a loan to their liege Lord or to do anything in that way through which anyone might on another occasion bring up against them that any of them had plotted against or deceived their said Lord, as heretofore was done in a similar case ; as in that of William de la Pole, Johan Wesenham, Johan Malewayn, Wauter Chiryton and of many other great merchants." [8] Lyons, Pecche and Bury were not mentioned, but the Londoners may well have been thinking of them when a man who had helped to lead the attack on them in the City was now mayor, and was using his power to attack the capitalists in every way he could.[9]

[1] It was still unrepaid in January 1381–82 (Cal. L.B.H, p. 160), but was probably paid by the June of that year (Cal. P.R. 1381–85, p. 149).

[2] Cal. P.R. 1381–85, p. 164.

[3] Ibid. p. 307. The sum lent was £2666 13s. 4d. A crown which formed part of the security for repayment was returned to the king, " at his earnest request," by Brembre in December 1383 (Cal. L.B.H, p. 219).

[4] A grocer.   [5] A mercer.   [6] A vintner.   [7] A grocer.

[8] Rot. Parl. III, p. 123.

[9] In the Parliament of the October following, Northampton attempted to get power to conduct usury trials (Rot. Parl. III, p. 142) which, according

Before Northampton's election in October 1381, however, the City and the country had to pass through June and the sudden flame of rebellion which June brought—the "Hurling tyme" as it is called in Gregory's Chronicle.[1] It is natural to expect that if the Londoners, or any section of them, bore a strong resentment against the Government, this resentment should have found expression in the Risings; further, the election of John of Northampton as mayor, which caused so many changes and so much disturbance in the City such a short while afterwards, is recorded as if it were accompanied by no conflict and no protest at the time; cannot this contradiction, perhaps, be explained by the effect which the incidents of the Risings had on the strength of the parties in London?

For the purpose of discovering the truth about these conjectures, the best account of what happened in London is to be found in the inquests taken at the trials of the rebels, whose findings can be supplemented by the lists of London rebels[2] to be found in the Rolls of Parliament[3] and the Plea and Memoranda Rolls of the City of London.[4] The accounts in the Chronicles do not give sufficient detail for it to be seen clearly how far the Londoners took the lead once the men of Kent and Essex had entered their City. Even when Londoners are mentioned there is scarcely any indication of what party or parties in London they represented, if any. The account of the Letter Book

to his accusers (Powell and Trevelyan, *Peasants' Rising and the Lollards*, p. 30) and the confession of his secretary (*London English*, 1384–1425, Chambers and Daunt, pp. 22–31), he intended to use to ruin the wealthier men of the City. It is not at all clear, however, what exactly were the powers he was trying to get. The City authorities had conducted such trials before (*Cal. L.B.G*, pp. 160–1, 162–3 and 267; *Cal. L.B.H*, pp. 23–4, 25–6), and Northampton himself had taken part in the last mentioned of these. See also *Rot. Parl.* III, pp. 280–1, for a petition in 1390 that the "good & profitable ordinance" made in the time of John Not, mayor of London (i.e. in 1363) against usury may be put into execution and that no "Seignur Espirituel" make any delay or disturbance of the correction of this horrible vice.

[1] p. 91.

[2] *C.R.R.* p. 488, partly printed and partly summarised by André Réville, *Le Soulèvement des travailleurs d'Angleterre en* 1381, pp. 190–241; these extracts are reprinted by Oman, *The Great Revolt of* 1381, pp. 206–13.

[3] *Rot. Parl.* III, pp. 112, 113.

[4] *Cal. P. and M.R.* 1364–81, pp. 288–91.

itself [1] omits so much—and such significant matters [2]—that it is impossible to believe that it was not censored with a purpose. The general tenor of the Chronicles, however, is confirmed by the inquisitions and the lists—the majority of the insurgents in London were from the lowest classes, and the entry of the rebels into the City meant for the ordinary Londoner an opportunity to get old grudges settled ; to take only one instance, the murder of Roger Legett, who was dragged from sanctuary at St. Martin's le Grand, and the burning of his property,[3] are not difficult to account for when we know that a few years before he had obtained a pardon [4] for putting " hidden engines of iron " in Fikettesfield,[5] so as to maim the clerks of Chancery, and the apprentices of the king's court, and others of the people of the City of London when they came to play there.

The inquisitions concern only twenty-two Londoners, the accusations against whom are set out in more or less detail, the largest amount of space by far being given to the misdoings of five aldermen, William Tonge, vintner, John Horn, fishmonger, Adam Karlille, grocer, John Fressh or Frossh, mercer, and Walter Sibil, fishmonger. Of the seventeen others, two have no occupation mentioned,[6] three are butchers, three brewers, two winedrawers, three drapers (of whom two were acquitted), one a saddler and one a goldsmith. This last, Thomas Farndon or Farringdon,

[1] Printed in Riley's *Memorials*, pp. 449-51.

[2] E.g. The treachery of Sibil, Horn, Tonge, Frossh, and Karlille, and the attempt to burn the " Jubile Book." In place of an account of the former it says of the rebels of Kent and Essex : " By the aid also of perfidious commoners within the City of their own condition, who rose in countless numbers there, they suddenly entered the City together," while it gives an impression of unanimous and enthusiastic loyalty in London after Wat Tyler's death.

[3] *Anom. Chron.* pp. 142 and 195. His fate may also have been due to his official position as " Grand Cisore," which Prof. Oman takes to mean Grand Assizer (*The Great Revolt*, p. 195 n.).

[4] *Cal. Cl.R.* 1374-77, pp. 210-11.

[5] This corresponds more or less to the modern Lincoln's Inn Fields (Williams, *Early Holborn*, pp. 38, 39).

[6] Theobald Elys and Paul Salesbury ; the latter's servant, Thomas, is on the list of those excepted from the general pardon (*Rot. Parl.* III, p. 113).

is the only one who bears a name of any note in the City.[1] His family had given several prominent members to the goldsmith's fraternity,[2] but his father was a bastard, and he had recently lost two law-suits, one certainly, and the other possibly, through this fact ; [3] some of his conduct during the Risings was confessedly due to his ejectment from a freehold tenement by the Prior of St. John of Jerusalem ; [4] he seized the king's bridle at his interview with the rebels at Mile End, calling upon him to avenge him of the false traitor prior, and is said to have been the chief of those who consented to his execution ; he is also accused of sitting up on the night of 13 June drawing up lists of citizens to be beheaded and turned out of their tenements, and he was in the act of destroying John Knot's tenement in Stanying Lane when he was captured.[5] Northampton's supporters at one time seem to have considered accusing Brembre of " maintaining " Farndon, but changed their minds.[6]

Paul Salesbury was the son of Sir Thomas Salesbury, knight, and had just come of age.[7] He came, " with many other evil-doers," to the house of William Baret, alderman, in St. Mary Bothaw, turned out Baret, his wife and servants, making him and his wife kneel to him in the street for a long while, and then give up to him the quitclaim to the property and a recognisance for a debt of £200 given by his father to Baret. They then went to the house of Hugh

---

[1] See Page, *London, its Origin and early Development*, pp. 181–2, for this family in the thirteenth and early fourteenth centuries and its connection with the ward of that name.

[2] Records of the Goldsmith's Coy. (unprinted) Wardens Accts. Book A, Part I, fos. 3 and 9.

[3] *Cal. Cl.R.* 1377-81, p. 177. *P. and M.R.* A24 m.5d. Réville, pp. 194-5.

[4] *Ibid.*

[5] Réville, p. 195. He also threatened to throw down the house of Gilbert Prynce, painter, in St. Giles without Cripplegate (*ibid.* p. 203) and is accused of destroying houses of the Prior of St. John at Cressing Temple and of demanding from the king a tenement of which he said he had been disseised by a certain Richard Weston (*ibid.* p. 204). It is somewhat surprising that he was pardoned in 1382, as innocent—at the request of the queen, the aldermen and mayor—i.e. Northampton (*Cal. P.R.* 1381-85, p. 103).

[6] See the confession of Northampton's secretary, Usk, printed in *London English*, pp. 26, 27.

[7] *Cal. L.B.H*, p. 170.

Fastolf in Thames Street and behaved in a similar fashion, seizing documents and weapons, using insults and threats, and drinking and wasting a great deal of wine and beer.[1] Of the other rebels, Adam atte Welle, butcher, is the most interesting. It was he, with another butcher, Roger Harry, who fourteen days before the rebels entered London, had incited the men of Essex to enter the City, and who, besides holding an unfortunate tailor to ransom for 20s., led the Essex men, with Harry again as his companion, against John of Gaunt's Palace of the Savoy;[2] having asserted this, the inquisition records without comment the amazing fact that he afterwards secured the position of a provider of victuals for the Lord Duke of Lancaster.[3]

The lists in the Rolls of Parliament and the Plea and Memoranda Rolls concern many more individuals—154 in the one case and 238 in the other—but they are merely lists of names; that in the Rolls of Parliament is of those who were excepted from the general pardon issued by the king to those accused of rebellion; in the Plea and Memoranda Rolls there are in reality two lists,[4] one being that presented by the alderman of each ward of those who were suspected of helping the rebels, containing 184 names, and the other, of 54 names, bearing no indication of its origin. To a considerable extent the lists in the City records and that in the Rolls of Parliament coincide.[5] They all point to the same conclusion, that the London rebels were drawn from the lowest classes,[6] and except in the case of the

---

[1] Réville, pp. 207–8. [2] *Ibid*. p. 196.

[3] *Ibid*. p. 198.

[4] On different membranes of the same roll. See *Cal. P. and M.R.* 1364–81, pp. 288–91 and 300.

[5] A table which shows to a certain extent the difference between them will be found in Appendix III.

[6] There is no further mention of them in the City records, as there would have been of at least some of them if they had held office or property of any value—and in connection with this it may be added that the indictment of Walter atte Key, brewer, of Woodstret, says that he fled, and had no chattels to confiscate (Réville, p. 206). Further, the surname of those whose occupations are not mentioned seem in many cases to be the name of the craft added to the Christian name of a man who has no family name, and some surnames are obviously nicknames, e.g. " Ricardus Vocatus Grete Richard, Diere " and " Laurentius Wyth te grete legg Sawyer."

weavers, whose object was to exterminate as many of their foreign competitors as possible, had no aim beyond that of plunder or private revenge. That they can represent a definite party in the City is incredible ; both victuallers and non-victuallers appear in the lists and though it may be argued that the latter are far more numerous there, according to the inquisitions the victuallers take the more prominent part, while a definite effort was made to burn the " Jubile Book," which, whatever else it may have contained, certainly included ordinances against victuallers.[1] None of Northampton's followers appear in the lists,[2] nor do their enemies ever accuse them of having taken part in the Risings—a thing they would surely have only been too glad to do if there had been any opportunity.

One accusation is made against one of Northampton's most prominent supporters, John More, concerning the rebellion, however, which, if it is true, is of considerable importance [3]—the accusation of having falsely accused Sibil, Horn and Karlille of treason, and of having suppressed all the evidence in their favour and sent up to the justices of the King's Bench only those inquisitions which would tell against them.[4] This, of course, could only have been done with the connivance of Northampton as mayor. There is much to support this accusation. That none of the aldermen returned their own names on their lists of suspects is perfectly comprehensible, but it is strange that their names nowhere appear in the City records as rebels or suspect rebels. In the Rolls of Parliament it is Sibil, Horn, and Karlille who are excepted from the general pardon—that is, the three whom the Northampton party is said to have accused falsely—while no mention is made

---

[1] The Walter atte Key mentioned above took part in this attempt (Réville, p. 206).

[2] It is perhaps worth noticing, however, that ten of the fifteen misteries, which later supported him—Pinners, Wiredrawers, Cardmakers, Curreours, Tilers, Smiths, Dyers, Fullers, Shearmen and Cordwainers—all lesser misteries—are represented (Powel and Trevelyan, *Peasants' Rising and the Lollards*, p. 27).

[3] And would be borne out by the entry in the Letter Book referred to above, p. 53, n. 2.

[4] *Peasants' Rising and the Lollards*, p. 30.

of Tonge and Frossh against whom, it is true, the evidence we have is not so strong, but who, together with the other three, are accused in the inquisitions to be found on the Coram Rege Roll. The assertion made at Northampton's trial is, to a very great extent, if not entirely, borne out by facts gathered from other sources. John More, mercer, was certainly the man who was responsible for bringing the five aldermen to trial, whatever may have been the part played by Northampton. Curiously enough, we find that he was bound over, on 31 July 1381, to keep the peace, and not to engage in "covins,"[1] though no mention is made of the recent risings in the record of the process.[2] No move was made against the five till October 1382. In the Parliament of that date were enacted the ordinances against the fishmongers which granted complete free trade to all foreign fishmongers, practically prevented London fishmongers from trading at all, and forbade any victuallers to hold judicial office in any town whatever.[3]

Walter Sibil[4] protested in Parliament against these petitions, before they became ordinances, declaring that the whole matter was being engineered by those who had been, in the past, imprisoned by Edward III's orders—these orders having been carried out by fishmongers who happened to

---

[1] This word can mean either a conspiracy, or a " cell " of associates—usually for objects likely to disturb the peace.

[2] *Cal. P. and M.R.* 1364–81, pp. 301–2 (a grocer, a chaplain, a shipwright, a joiner, a tailor, a shearman, a squire, a taverner, a corsour, a weaver and two other persons were bound over at the same time).

[3] *Rot. Parl.* III, p. 141. Exton appealed to the king on behalf of the fishmongers, whereupon Northampton declared that never in his life had he seen the City so in " unnitee amour et concorde " but for the fishmongers who were endeavouring to maintain their extortions from and oppression of the people (*ibid.* p. 143).

[4] It would no doubt be shockingly anachronistic to speak of " billingsgate " in the fourteenth century, but Sibil's irrepressible tongue makes him a worthy fore-runner of his seventeenth-century counterparts. Not only does it get him into trouble here, but three years later he earned three years' imprisonment for saying that Robert de Vere had maintained Nicholas Twyford in a law-suit against himself (*Rot. Parl.* III, pp. 186 and 399–400)—the case was still dragging on in 1391 (*ibid.* p. 298)—while in 1388, when the king's ambassador in Prussia, he offended a representative of the Grand Master of the Teutonic Order so much that the Grand Master made a formal complaint to Richard II (Lists and Indexes, xlix ; Diplomatic documents Nos. 1638 and 1643.)

be " the principal officials of the City " at that time.[1] The
incident he referred to was in May 1371 when Northampton
and three of his followers [2] were arrested and imprisoned
in the Tower, with eight others unconnected with his party.
Sibil, however, was exaggerating about the fishmongers,
because though Walworth was one of the sheriffs, the other,
Robert Cayton, was the Common Serjeant of the City,
and therefore a lawyer, while the mayor [3] was a mercer and
only two of the aldermen, besides Walworth, were fishmongers.[4] His speech provoked a storm, for John More,
one of the members for the City,[5] thereupon declared that
the City was well able to defend itself against all the
fishmongers, even if they brought in again the Commons of
Essex and Kent. Sibil then demanded that More should
explain himself more fully ; the latter then replied that it
was Sibil, Horn and Karlille who prevented Walworth
from keeping out the rebels, and claimed an " official
enquiry," which was granted. The trial followed that autumn
or winter before Adam Bamme and John Sely, sheriffs,[6]
but of it we have no record except the inquisitions [7] which
were brought from it before the King's Bench the following
Easter. The story we gather from them is briefly as follows :
Before the men of Kent and Essex entered the City, while
they were at Greenwich and Blackheath on 12 June, Horn,
Frossh and Karlille had been sent by the mayor to persuade
them, if possible, to depart ; Horn, on the contrary, with
the consent of Karlille and Frossh, encouraged the rebels,
and even brought back several of their leaders into the City
and lodged them that night in his house. Later Horn
procured a standard and rode out to Blackheath to encourage
the rebels there, quarrelling on the way with a certain
John Blyton [8] who had been sent by the king with a message

---

[1] *Rot. Parl.* III, p. 143.   [2] Essex, More and William Norton.

[3] John Bernes.   [4] For the whole incident see *Cal. L.B.G*, p. 281.

[5] Northampton's secretary, Usk, in his confession mentioned above, p. 54,
n. 6, declared Northampton had chosen the members for this Parliament
himself.

[6] They had been elected on 21 September (*Cal. L.B.H*, pp. 197–8).

[7] Reville, pp. 190–9, *Great Revolt*, pp. 206–13.

[8] Later one of Northampton's followers, and imprisoned for his loyalty
to him (see Appendix IV). Blyton wished to know Horn's message

to the same band of rebels ; when the mob had entered London, Horn seized the opportunity to pay off old scores in favour of his friends, forcing Robert Norton, tailor, to pay £10 to a John Pecche, fishmonger, and turning Richard Toky, grocer, out of his tenement in Lumbard Street in favour of Matilla Toky.[1] According to the inquisition, the men of Kent had been let in over London Bridge on 13 June by Walter Sibil, alderman of Bridge, who refused the help Thomas Cornwaleys would have brought him, and said the Kentishmen were the citizens' friends and the king's. Those of Essex had already been let in through Aldgate by William Tonge, alderman of that ward, during the night between the 12 and 13 June. Further, on the 15th, when Wat Tyler was lying dead in Smithfield and Walworth was attempting to raise a force within the City to go to Richard's rescue, it was Sibil and Horn who called on the citizens to shut their gates and allow no one to enter or leave the City, because the rebels had killed both the king and the mayor. In a second inquisition, taken on 4 November, it is declared that Horn, in negotiating treacherously with the rebels, was acting apart from Karlille and Frossh, and that the jurors cannot determine whether Tonge, in opening Aldgate, was acting intentionally treacherously or from fear of what the rebels would do if he refused them entrance. The names of the jurors are not given by Réville, but they appear on the roll itself, and it is very significant that only one [2] of the second jury, but no less than ten [3] of the first, appear nearly three years later in the list of supporters of John of Northampton given at his trial.[4]

The accused were given bail till November 1383, then further bail was given till January 1383–84, when it was demanded whether anyone had anything to say against them ; no one appeared, and a fresh jury (whose members are not

from the City, so that it should agree with his own from the king—but Horn told him to mind his own business, and that he should say what he pleased (Réville, p. 191).

[1] *Ibid.* pp. 192–3.   [2] Robert Yorke.

[3] Will. Tyngewyk, Robt. Fraunceys, Robert Pipot, John Hydyngham, John Wylby, John Wyllardby, John Cole, Thomas Depham, Thomas Kyngesbrugge and John Dancastre.

[4] See Appendix IV.

named) declared them innocent. This occurred when Brembre had been mayor for three months, and only a few weeks before Northampton's arrest.[1] On the other hand, we have evidence that the capitalists did what they could in their favour, for Horn was released from the Tower in March 1382–83 on mainprise of Philpot and Walworth, as were also Karlille, Sibil and Tonge,[2] while a considerable number of lesser people were pardoned later at the request of Nicholas Exton.[3] Horn is the only one of the five of whom no later record than that of his release appears to exist. John Fresshe was elected alderman[4] of Cordwainer Street annually from 1385–94, when annual elections ceased, and became mayor in October 1394 ;[5] Adam Karlille was similarly elected alderman of Aldgate[6] in 1390, 1391 and 1393, he was sheriff in 1388[7] and M.P. for the City in 1388,[8] 1390[9] and 1395 ;[10] William Tonge was deputy alderman of Tower in 1384,[11] alderman of Tower the next year,[12] and M.P. for the City in 1388.[13] Though Walter Sibil was never again a full alderman, Walworth appointed him his deputy in Bridge in 1384,[14] he was a member of the Common Council in that year,[15] and we find him summoned in 1388 to attend the King's Council to treat of " business which concerns the estate of the realm,"[16] while a few months later (as has been mentioned above) he is termed the king's ambassador to Prussia.[17]

What conclusions may be drawn from all this ? It seems probable that John Horn was the only one of the five who was deliberately a traitor—he certainly used the opportunities given him by the presence of the rebels in the City for his own personal ends,[18] and was unwilling to lose the position

[1] 9 February 1383–84 (*Cal. Cl.R.* 1381–85, p. 369).
[2] *Ibid.* p. 284.
[3] *Cal. P.R.* 1385–89, pp. 280, 349 ; *ibid.* 1389–92, pp. 25 and 290, etc.
[4] *Cal. L.B.H*, pp. 263, 284, 304, 325, 341, 352, 362.
[5] *Ibid.* p. 417.   [6] *Ibid.* pp. 352, 362 and 393.
[7] *Ibid.* p. 332.   [8] *Ibid.* p. 286.   [9] *Ibid.* p. 349.
[10] *Ibid.* p. 417.   [11] *Ibid.* p. 247.   [12] *Ibid.* p. 263.
[13] *Ibid.* p. 329.   [14] *Ibid.* p. 247.
[15] *Cal. P. and M.R.* 1381–1412, p. 86.
[16] *Cal. Cl.R.* 1385–98, p. 388.
[17] *Ibid.* p. 403. *Cal. P.R.* 1385–98, p. 453.
[18] None of the others is accused of this.

of power he had gained, when Walworth called the City to arms after the death of Wat Tyler. The other four aldermen were probably afraid of the consequences of refusing entrance to the men of Kent and Essex. If they had been forced by the mob within to open the gates to the mob without, instead of doing so with a show of willingness, something like a sack of London might have followed. If they did reason in this way, it would have been an argument which would certainly have appealed to the capitalist class, who do not seem to have disapproved of their conduct.[1] One of the acts of the rebels in Southwark indeed—the attack on the Marshalsea—must have pleased all London after the events of 1377. It is, in fact, implied in the inquisition taken 1382 that it was due to the encouragement of Horn, Karlille and Frossh.[2] It is doubtful whether there was even much disapproval when the marshal, Richard Imworth,[3] was dragged from sanctuary at Westminster and murdered.[4]

It is clear that the attack on the Savoy was not directed by any particular party in London, though Northampton may have later impressed upon John of Gaunt that it had occurred when the party opposed to him was in power, as he certainly used the incidents of the Risings as a means of ruining, temporarily at least, some of the prominent " victuallers."

It is more difficult to determine in what way the Risings affected the mayoralty elections in October 1381 ; it is probable, however, that the aldermen would be eager to avoid a disputed election which would give opportunitites for popular demonstrations and riots ; perhaps, too, Northampton's attitude was not quite realised ; he acted very cautiously at first, not even revoking the judgment passed against his supporters in 1377, when they had been expelled from the Council,[5] till February 1381–82,[6] and not acting against the fishmongers for a year.[7]

---

[1] They themselves seem to have been members of this class though not in the first rank of wealth.

[2] " hillares devenerunt . . . et carcerem domini regis vocatum le Marchalsye ffregerunt."

[3] " homme saunz pite come tourmentour," *Anom. Chron.* p. 146.

[4] Réville, p. 212.   [5] *Cal. L.B.H*, p. 34. See above, p. 26.

[6] *Ibid.* p. 176.   [7] *Rot. Parl.* III, pp. 141 ff.

If the capitalists had realised how bitter was his enmity against them, they perhaps would have risked a riot at election time ; but they must have been conscious that the next riot might very probably have been directed definitely against them as a class—whilst in June they had only suffered individually from personal spite,[1] or from their connection with the Government.[2] It was not until they had recognised what his ends were, and how difficult it was to prevent him attaining them, so long as he was mayor, that they dared face the possibility of election disturbances.

[1] Some of these cases have been described already—but Brembre also suffered, from a William Treweman, brewer, who seized his bridle as he rode beside the king, railing on him for injuries done while he was mayor, and later came to his house in the Riole, and forced him, for fear of the mob with him, to hand him over 5 marks. It was not, however, only the rich who suffered.

[2] Cf. the murder of Lyons by the Londoners with the wrecking of his manor at Overall which was the first act of the rebels under Wrawe. " The Rising in Suffolk " (*Trans. Royal Hist. Soc. N.S. VIII*, p. 211), John Bucturwike, called Doget, Sub-Sheriff of Middlesex, whose house at Westminster was burnt by the rebels, was the son of Walter Doget, vintner, and the husband of Idonea Birlingham, step-daughter of Philpot (*Anom. Chron.* ; Réville, p. 210–11 ; *Cal. P. and M.R.* 1381–1412, p. 103 ; *Cal. Wills*, II, p. 354 ; *Cal. L.B.H*, p. 49).

CHAPTER V

JOHN OF NORTHAMPTON AND THE CITY

THE man who became mayor in October 1381 stands out
for us in the pages of Walsingham[1] keen-witted and stout-
hearted, proud and resolute of purpose. The continuator
of Higden[2] describes him as one who filled his office of mayor
with firmness and inflexibility. His following, according to
Walsingham, was almost the entire community of London;[3]
the continuator of Higden practically defines his party as
consisting of those opposed to the monopoly of the free
fishmongers,[4] and this is the view which survived in London
tradition.[5] Walsingham implies that he was in some sense
a follower of Wiclif; he describes in detail the proceedings
taken by Northampton and the Londoners during his
mayoralty against persons openly guilty of immorality, and
adds: "For they were also inspired by John Wiclif and were
his followers to carry things out in this way in censure
of the Prelates."[6] Further on he describes the trial of Master
John Aston, a follower of Wiclif, conducted by the Archbishop of Canterbury during Northampton's mayoralty,[7]
which was violently interrupted by the Londoners, who broke

---

[1] *Hist. Anglic.* p. 65. The passage is identical with *Chron. Ang.* pp.
349–50.

[2] Higden, ix, p. 29. (If, as seems probable, this continuation is by a monk
of Westminster, it is of considerable value for London affairs. See note in
bibliography).

[3] *Hist. Anglic.* II, p. 65. *Chron. Ang.* p. 350.

[4] Higden, IX, p. 29, n. 5.

[5] See above, p. 27. Many of the fifteenth and sixteenth-century chronicles
do not menion more than his name on the list of mayors, e.g. Julius B.II
(*Chronicles of London*, ed. Kingsford), and those which copy this. Many
do not begin till 1400.

[6] *Hist. Ang.* II, p. 65; *Chron. Ang.* p. 349. Some modern writers assume
that Northampton led a "democratic" party, and some that all non-victuallers were his followers. Neither of these views seems to be supported by
the evidence.

[7] *Hist. Ang.* II, p. 66.

in the doors of the room in which the trial was taking place. The mayor himself is not alluded to and no names are mentioned, but there are certainly no records of the City authorities punishing or binding over anyone concerned in such a breach of the peace. Walsingham does not, on the other hand, connect Northampton with the interruption of Wiclif's trial at Lambeth in 1378, which was due, so he says, not to the citizens but to the rabble of London,[1] who forced themselves into the chapel and defended the accused. The continuator of Higden, though he goes into considerable detail about Northampton's career,[2] connects him in no way with Wiclif and makes no reference to his action against immorality. The continuator of Knighton [3] does not once mention Northampton's name, but he describes a procession of clerks and laymen through the City, in the early summer of 1382, the second year of Northampton's mayoralty, to mark the occasion of the condemnation of Wiclif's opinion on the Blessed Sacrament, and makes no suggestion at all that the Londoners favoured the Lollard.

The City records[4] certainly bear out Walsingham's account of a campaign against immorality carried on while Northampton was mayor, a campaign which, without doubt, was a direct attack on the jurisdiction of the Church Courts in such matters, and was, therefore, inspired by " Lollardy " in one sense of that term. It would be extremely difficult to maintain, however, that this attitude towards Ecclesiastical Courts was peculiar to one man or to one party in London. Instances which show how widespread it was and of what long standing, have been given in an earlier chapter.[5] Not even action against open immorality was an innovation. As far back as 1296 [6] the king had seen cause to interfere to prevent the arrest and imprisonment of adulterous ecclesiastics by the City officers. The regulations of 1382[7] as to the dress of women of ill-fame only reproduce those of 1351 ;[8] while the ordinances establishing

---

[1] *Hist. Ang.* I, p. 356. *Chron. Ang.* p. 183.
[2] Higden, pp. 29, 30 and 45–9.   [3] Knighton, II, p. 163.
[4] *Cal. L.B.H*, pp. 176 and 189.   [5] See above, pp. 15–16.
[6] *Lib. Cust.* I, p. 213.   [7] *Cal. L.B.H*, p. 176.
[8] *Cal. L.B.F*, p. 241.

" la peyne contre putours baudes prestres et advoutours,"
which is undated but which, because of its place in the
Letter Book [1] appears to belong to the summer of 1382,
met with no opposition from Northampton's enemies, and
remained in force at least until the compilation of the
Liber Albus in 1419,[2] although his party had very little
influence in the City after 1383.

Northampton also took action to prevent the poor
from being forced to offer more than they could afford at
baptisms, marriages and requiems;[3] it was alleged that
the offerings of wealthier people set a standard which the
poor were forced to imitate at a rate which was excessive;
henceforward no one was to offer more than a " ferlyng "
at Masses for the dead, and nothing at all if he who received
the offering refused to give change, while those who offered
more than a certain amount at baptisms or marriages were
to be fined. The mayor's motive may be interpreted as
genuine compassion for the poor, or a desire to attract
popularity or a mixture of both, according to one's view of
his character. At the best his " Lollardy " was of Lang-
land's type,[4] at the worst he was acting from worldly rather
than heretical motives. He certainly had no sympathy
with Wiclif's attack on Church property and chantries, for
in his will he founded a chantry in St. Mary de Elsyngspitel[5]
and left property to the nuns of Holy Trinity, Cheshunt,
on condition that his name and those of his parents and others
should be on their bead-roll, and the remainder of lands

---

[1] *Cal. L.B.H*, p. 189.

[2] *Liber Albus*, I, pp. 457–60. One such case of 1389 is described, *Cal. P. and
M.R.* 1381–1412, p. 148, another, of 1395, *ibid.* p. 228, the latter concerning
members of religious orders. See also an interesting case in January 1388–89
where it is declared that in accordance with the custom of the City a chaplain
and a woman guilty of adultery were handed over to the Ordinary, because
no one had appeared to prosecute in the City Courts, though due notice had
been given (*Cal. L.B.H*, p. 339).

[3] *Memorials*, p. 463.

[4] See particularly Passus I, lines 188–197, where he speaks of the chaplains
who " chewen here charite and chiden after more." " Thei ben acom-
bred with covetise. Thei konne nouzt don it fram hem so hard hath auarice
yhasped hem togidere."

[5] Situated where is the modern Spital Square.

to the Charterhouse on the same condition.[1] Such wills of his supporters that we possess have similar provisions.[2]

Excommunication for secular purposes, which was also attacked by Wiclif, does not seem to have given rise to any dispute between the City and Church authorities at this time, though there is very little doubt that no mayor, of whatever party, would have approved of it.[3]

If, however, Northampton's policy towards the Church was not one which divided the City, the same can decidedly not be said of his secular policy. It is possible to state in some detail what kind of men supported him in this. In the inquisitions taken at the ex-mayor's trial are to be found the names of fifty-four of his most prominent supporters ;[4] of these, five were subsequently acquitted,[5] while a sixth[6] is only accused of having ranged himself on the side of Northampton up to the time of Brembre's election as mayor. In the Plea and Memoranda Rolls there is a list of persons bound over on account of various disturbances connected with the election of Brembre and the defeat and subsequent arrest of Northampton.[7] Some of the names are identical with those to be found in the inquisitions on the Coram Rege Roll, but there are, in addition, the names

---

[1] There are other legacies to various altars and chaplains, and to the monks of the Charterhouse—in this last case to provide them each with ½lb. of ginger and 1lb. of dates, raisins and figs, over their usual pittance in Lent (*Cal. Wills*, II, pp. 333–5. Court of London, Courtenay, fos. 406–7)

[2] John Carbonell founded a chantry in St. Vedast (*Cal. Wills*, II, p. 365) ; Thomas Noket one in St. Mary Wolnoth (*ibid.* p. 323), while Thomas Carleton left a rent charge for the maintenance of a chantry in St. John Baptist's Chapel within the north gate of St. Paul's, and vestments, apparel for the altar and altar vessels for the same Chapel (*ibid.* p. 272).

[3] There are two cases in Letter Book G—both apparently in 1365—in one of which the king forbids the parson of St. Mary Wolchirchhawe to excommunicate the wardens of London Bridge for letting to ferm the stalls and benches at " les stokkes," which he had claimed belonged to his Church (*Cal. L.B.G*, pp. 194 and 199).

[4] Powell and Trevelyan, *Peasant's Rising and the Lollards*, pp. 27–38 and Appendix IV.

[5] J. Maudelyn, R. Riseby, W. Norton, J. Cheddar and J. Vyne—the acquittal seems to rest on a legal technicality (*Cal. P. and M.R. 1381–1412*, pp. 136–8).

[6] Adam Bamme. See particularly Usk's confession (*London English*, p. 29).

[7] *Cal. P. and M.R. 1381–1412*, pp. 57–68.

of eighty-five men who are not so mentioned. Of these one hundred and thirty-nine persons only nine are undescribed in any way.[1] Of the remaining one hundred and thirty-two, one only belongs to a victualling mistery—Richard Molle, grocer.[2] This in itself is certainly a striking proof that those who supported Northampton were non-victuallers, but other considerations make it inappropriate to give them the title of " the non-victualling party."[3] Chief among these considerations is the number of aldermen belonging to non-victualling misteries who do not appear in any list of Northampton's supporters, and who made no recorded effort on his behalf, however far they may have acquiesced in his general policy while he was mayor. Of the aldermen in office when Northampton was elected mayor, and for five months afterwards, ten[4] belonged to non-victualling misteries[5]—three were drapers,[6] three were mercers,[7] two skinners,[8] one a goldsmith[9] and one a tailor;[10] none of them was ever accused of supporting Northampton. In the following March,[11] twelve non-victuallers were elected—Northampton himself, two of his undoubted supporters, Thomas Carleton, " broderer," and John More, mercer, Adam Bamme, goldsmith, who later joined the party opposed to him, and three skinners,[12] two drapers,[13] two mercers[14] and an armourer,[15] who were not connected with his party at all. At the time of Brembre's election

---

[1] Ric. Yoman, Michael Hakeneye, John Covewell, Will. Maxwell, John Whyte, Roger Wygemor (acquitted), William Sheryngham (acquitted), Simon Stratton and John Whytyngdon.

[2] *Cal. P. and M.R.* 1381–1412, p. 62. A grocer, William Mayhew, was, however, punished in May 1384 for saying that the City was badly and unjustly governed and that John Constantyn had been falsely condemned to death (*ibid.* p. 50).

[3] As is often done.

[4] The aldermen were elected 12 March, the mayor 13 October.

[5] *Cal. L.B.H*, pp. 163–4.

[6] J. Hende, W. Kyng and R. Boxford.

[7] J. Heylesdone, J. Boseham and J. Fresshe.

[8] W. Knightcote, and Th. Irlond.

[9] R. Lucas.   [10] J. Redynge.   [11] *Cal. L.B.H*, pp. 177–8.

[12] W. Wodehous, J. Rote and J. Sely.

[13] Hervey Begge and J. Walcote.

[14] J. Organ and J. Eston.   [15] Simon Wynchecombe.

and of Northampton's arrest, out of fifteen aldermen [1] belonging to the non-victualling misteries—seven mercers,[2] three goldsmiths,[3] three drapers [4] and two skinners [5]—only two, Richard Norbury and Thomas Noket, were followers of Northampton, while Boseham, Warbulton, Fresshe, Rote, Fraunceis, Wynchecombe, and Hende were members of the body who petitioned for his execution in March 1384–85.[6] The total number of non-victuallers holding the office of alderman during the three years from March 1380–81 to March 1383–84 was thirty-five,[7] only six of whom can be said to be of Northampton's party—including Northampton himself and Bamme, of whom Northampton's secretary said, " truly Adam Bamme was noght so comunly ne so bysy on thys purpos . . . as waire the tother," and claimed that he ceased to support Northampton when the latter ceased to be mayor.[8] It might be argued, and has indeed, been assumed,[9] that Nicholas Twyford, goldsmith, was a follower of Northampton, but if he were, it is very difficult to account for the absence of his name from the inquisitions taken at the ex-mayor's trial. It is true that his relations with Brembre were far from cordial. On the Sunday in 1378 when, out of the " rancour " between the goldsmiths and the pepperers, a great affray arose " while the Bishop of Carlisle was preaching in St. Paul's Church-yard ; in which place because of such conflict and the wounded fleeing thither with very great outcry, no little tumult and alarm ensued,"[10] Twyford, then sheriff, obstructed

---

[1] *Cal. L.B.H*, pp. 213–4.

[2] J. Boseham, J. Heylesdone, R. Warbulton, W. Anecroft, J. Shadeworth, W. Shiryngham and Ric. Norbury.

[3] H. Bamme, J. Fraunceis, and N. Twyford.

[4] Th. Noket, W. Kyng and J. Furneux.

[5] W. Olyver and Th. Rolf.

[6] *Cal. P. and M.R.* 1381–1412, p. 54.

[7] Two mercers and one draper aldermen in 1380–81 were re-elected after the compulsory years interval.

[8] *London English*, pp. 29, 30 ; cf. *Cal. L.B.H*, pp. 237–44. Bamme later married Philpot's widow, Stodeye's daughter Margaret (*Cal. P.R.* 1396–99, p. 376).

[9] By Prof. Pollard in his article on Twyford in the *D.N.B.* and Dr. Sharpe, *London and the Kingdom*, i, p. 239.

[10] *Memorials*, pp. 415–6.

Brembre as mayor, in the arrest of a certain man[1] who accompanied him to a meeting called by Brembre to deal with the riot. For his disobedience and rudeness Brembre deprived him for a short time of his shrievalty and forced him to give surety for good behaviour. This recognisance was not cancelled till the mayoralty of Northampton.[2] Further, according to the continuator of Higden,[3] Twyford put himself forward as a candidate for the mayoralty in October 1384, and was only defeated by Brembre by means of armed men concealed by the latter in the Guildhall. A London chronicler says they were partly " men of the contre at Harowe and the contre there aboughte,"[4] which looks as if they may have been tenants of Brembre's.[5] A very similar account of this election is given in the petitions of several of the non-victualling misteries to the Parliament of 1386 against Brembre, and his successor in office, Exton.[6] It is noticeable, however, that Twyford is not mentioned in these petitions, and that there was not one presented by his own mistery, that of the goldsmiths. It may be granted that he was probably a rival of Brembre, but that rivalry alone cannot be said to make him a follower, or even an ally, of Northampton.

None of the latter's followers, indeed, held such a prominent position in the City as Twyford.[7] Northampton

---

[1] John Worsele—his gild is not mentioned.

[2] March 1381–82 (*Cal. L.B.H*, p. 99; *Memorials*, pp. 415–7).

[3] Higden, IX, pp. 50–1.

[4] Harleian, 565, p. 76.

[5] See above Chapter I, p. 4. He had land both at Harrow (*Cal. P.R.* 1385–89, p. 478) and Ruislip (MS. *Cal. Inquis. p.m.* III, p. 110, no. 172). This chronicle does not mention Twyford's claim.

[6] *Rot. Parl.* III, pp. 225–7, where those of the Mercers and Cordwainers are printed. That of the Drapers is printed by Johnson in his history of the Coy. I, pp. 208–11. That of the Cutlers (which is also that of the Bowyers, Fleichers, Esporiours and Bladesmyths) is printed and translated in Welch's history of that Coy. I, pp. 263–71, and that of the Saddlers (but in modern English) in J. W. Sherwell's *History of the Saddlers Coy.*, pp. 41 ff. The others are of the Embroiderers [*Ancient Petitions* (1000)], Founders (1002), Armourers (1005), Leathersellers (1001) Painters (1004) and Pinners (1003).

[7] An indication of his importance as a goldsmith is the fact that when the City made a present to the Black Prince in 1371 £188 10s. 2d. worth of goods was bought, as part of it, from Twyford (*Memorials*, p. 351). John of Gaunt often bought plate from him (J. of G.'s Register *passim*).

himself [1] was a man of position and of considerable, though not of great wealth. His supporters were insignificant in both respects. Setting aside Bamme, only four [2] of them ever held the office of alderman, if we except John Vyne, who was afterwards declared innocent of aiding him. None of these four held the office before the period of annual elections, two of them only held it for one year; [3] two for two years; [4] John More alone held the office of sheriff, and he was elected by Northampton himself; [5] apart from William Essex who had been M.P. for the City in 1370 [6] and 1376 [7] and perhaps, though not very probably, in 1357 [8] and 1358, [9] and Geoffrey Waldern [10] who was M.P. in 1395, it is only while Northampton is mayor that the City is represented by his supporters—by More, Carleton, Essex and Norbury in October 1382, [11] and More, Norbury and Essex in February 1382–83. [12] Of the rest of his followers, ten [13] at one time or another served as common councillors, as did also Geoffrey Waldern [14]—seven of them being members of the council of 1376, [15] which disfranchised John Pecche of which council Norbury, More and Essex were

[1] See above, Chapter I.

[2] Ric. Norbury, Th. Noket, J. More and Th. Carleton. This man had probably been the King's armourer under Edward III. Devon : Issue Roll of Thomas de Brantingham 6 : 460, etc.

[3] Norbury and More.

[4] Noket and Carleton. The last alone was ever alderman after Northampton's defeat. See Beaven, I.

[5] *Cal. L.B.H*, p. 218 (one sheriff at this time was always chosen by the mayor, the other by the commonalty).

[6] *Cal. L.B.G*, p. 275.　　　　　　　[7] *Cal. L.B.H*, p. 20.

[8] *Cal. L.B.G*, p. 82.　　　　　　　[9] *Ibid.* p. 94.

[10] *Cal. L.B.H*, p. 417.　　　　　　[11] *Ibid.* p. 198.

[12] *Ibid.* p. 211. Brembre was the fourth member sitting as an alderman, as did John More. They were the first members, so far as we have record, to be elected in a Common Council held at the Guildhall. (See McKesack, *Representation of Eng. Boroughs in the Middle Ages*, pp. 130–2.)

[13] J. Carbonell (1376 and July 1384), J. Doncaster (coppersmith), 1376 and 1388, Th. Lincolle (draper), July and October 1384, July 1385 and 1388, J. Wilby (tailor), July 1385, Robert Pipot (bowyer), J. Hydyngham (hatter), W. Belhomme (leathermonger) and Robt. Franceys (goldsmith), 1376, J. Longe (cordwainer), 1376 and July 1384, and Ric. Brendewoode (draper) 1388.

[14] June and July 1384 and March and July 1385. The dates show their attendance.

[15] *Cal. L.B.H*, pp. 42–4. For the other councils see Appendix II.

also members. Of the financial position of his followers it is almost impossible to discover anything, which points to the conclusion that they were men of moderate, if not indeed of small, means. This is confirmed by the list of those who contributed to the £600 spent by the City in 1379 in conciliating the lords, which, although it contains a hundred and sixty-eight names, only includes those of three of Northampton's supporters; one of these, Thomas Noket, contributed £4, and the other two, Waldern and Norbury, five marks each.[1] From their wills it can be seen that Carleton,[2] Carbonell[3] and Noket[4] held a fair amount of property in the City, but the absence of wills of any other of Northampton's followers points to the possession of very little real or personal property on their part. It must not be thought, however, that Northampton's party consisted of men of no account in the misteries they represented, for there is evidence that sixteen of them—William Essex[5] and Guy Paulyn, drapers,[6] John Cole[7] and Thomas Depham,[8] saddlers, Richard Norbury,[9] mercer, William Belhomme,[10] leathermonger, Thomas Kyngsbrigge,[11] John Remes,[12] John Longe, junior,[13] and Robert Yorke,[14] cordwainer, John Wilby,[15] tailor, and John Carbonell,[16] William Tyngewyk,[17] Stephen Thorp,[18] Robert

---

[1] *Cal. L.B.H*, pp. 124–6.   [2] *Cal. of Wills*, ii, p. 272.

[3] *Ibid.* p. 365.

[4] *Ibid.* pp. 322–3. Noket also possessed the manor of " Rislepe " and lands and tenements in " Colesdon."

[5] 1364, *Cal. P. and M.R. 1323–64*, p. 267.

[6] 1378, *Cal. L.B.H*, p. 79.   [7] 1376, *ibid.* p. 35.

[8] 1388–89, *P. and M.R.* A28 m.15 (uncalendared).

[9] 1397, *Cal. P.R. 1396–99*, p. 109.

[10] 1372, *Cal. L.B.G*, p. 293.

[11] 1375 and 1389, *Cal. L.B.H*, pp. 18 and 346.

[12] 1375, *ibid.* p. 18.   [13] 1375, *ibid.*

[14] 1386, *ibid.* p. 291. He is among those who lead the attack on the serving-men's fraternity. *Ibid.* p. 311, see above, p. 16.

[15] 1388–89. *P. and M.R.* A29, m.1 (uncalendared).

[16] 1373, 1377, 1382, 1400; Goldsmiths' Records (unpublished), Wardens' Accts. and Court Minutes Book A, Pt. i, fos. 49, 59 ; Pt. ii, fos. 21 and 33.

[17] 1355, 1367, 1369, 1373, 1382, *ibid.* Pt. i, fos. 12, 34, 38, 49, 59.

[18] 1383, 1390, 1399, *ibid.* Pt. i, fos. 73 and 85 ; Pt. ii, fo. 29.

Franceys[1] and John Lincoln,[2] goldsmiths—held at one time or another the position of warden of their respective misteries, or a position corresponding to it in powers if not in name. If the wardens' accounts of more of the misteries existed for this period, probably the list would be considerably lengthened. It may well be that the most prominent men in any mistery left the fulfilment of the duties of warden to the members of average wealth—the small masters in fact—when their own business increased and when they took upon themselves the more important duties of alderman, sheriff and mayor. Nicholas Twyford and Adam Bamme, for example, the two most notable goldsmiths of the reign of Richard II, were not wardens of their gild later than 1374 and 1377 respectively. [3] Nicholas Brembre and John Philpot, again, do not appear to have served as wardens after 1369,[4] but as the grocers' records are incomplete,[5] certainty on this point is impossible.

With regard to personal details about Northampton's followers, it is clear that many of them had already come into conflict with the City authorities, and on this account probably bore them a grudge. As early as 1371, Essex and More, together with Northampton himself and nine other persons [6] had been sent to the Tower by the sheriffs, by order of the king, because the peace of the City had been disturbed.[7] In 1377 Essex and More, with Richard Norbury, John Willarby and Robert Fraunceys, were expelled from the Common Council for betraying its secrets.[8] Robert

---

[1] 1369, 1390, *ibid.* Pt. I, fos. 38 and 79.

[2] 1377, *ibid.* Pt. II, fo. 21.

[3] Twyford was warden in 1365, 1371 and 1374, *ibid.* Pt. I, fos. 31, 34, 45 and 50, and A. Bamme in 1372 and 1377, *ibid.* Pt. I, fo. 47 ; Pt. II, fo. 21.

[4] *Grocers' Coy. Records*, I, 42 and Kingdon MS. I, p. 122.

[5] There are no wardens' lists for 1375–78, 1380–82 or 1384. This company provided that no one should be made to serve a second time as warden till after the lapse of seven years " as it is laborowse to hem that ben Wardenez." Kingdon MS. I, 122, quoted by Dr. Thrupp in her unprinted thesis on the grocers. It is curious that Philpot's name is not in the list of members for 1373 (*Grocers' Coy. Records*, I, p. 45).

[6] Including Will. Norton, who was later accused of helping Northampton, but was afterwards acquitted.

[7] *Cal. L.B.G*, p. 281, see above, Chapter IV, p. 58.

[8] *Cal. L.B.H*, p. 64, see above, p. 26, n. 7 and 8,

Fraunceys, indeed, seems to have been of very doubtful character, for, not only had he received a pardon,[1] " at the supplication of the king's uncle, John duke of Lancaster," for the death of " Peter atte Nether-lond," but later, in 1395, he was accused of a share in the murder of a London citizen, Robert Baroun, horner.[2] John Hydyngham, hatter, John Wilughbi or Willarby, tailor, and John Muntham, joiner,[3] had been convicted in 1379, before Philpot, then mayor, of maintaining plaints and " frequenting the Courts of the mayor and sheriffs for the time being, without cause, to the obstruction of the law." [4] Essex had been convicted of threatening the jurors in a case in 1370,[5] while Thomas Lincolle,[6] John More,[7] William Waldrian,[8] Thomas Carleton,[9] Robert Fraunceys,[10] John Feraunt [11] and Richard Norbury [12] had all, at one time or another, been bound over to keep the peace, as indeed, had Northampton himself.[13]

Such were the men who, at Northampton's trial, were accused of having favoured his policy as mayor and of having created riot and disturbance in the City when he failed to be re-elected. The lists in the Plea and Memoranda Rolls in which many of their names reappear, are concerned with disturbances which occurred after Northampton's arrest,[14] and more especially with those which took place

[1] As mentioned above, p. 27, n. 3.

[2] *Cal. P. and M.R.* 1381–1412, p. 234.

[3] Also William Norton, saddler.

[4] *Cal. L.B.H*, pp. 112–15.   [5] *Cal. L.B.G*, p. 273.

[6] In 1369, *Cal. P. and M.R.* 1364–81, p. 111.

[7] *Ibid.* and in 1376–77 ; *ibid.* p. 241 and 1381 ; *ibid.* p. 301.

[8] 1364, *ibid.* 1323–64, p. 273, and 1373, *ibid.* 1364–81, p. 151 (names uncalendared).

[9] 1364, *P. and M.R.* A10, m.14d. (uncalendared).

[10] 1366, *Cal. P. and M.R.* 1364–81, p. 71.

[11] 1369, *ibid.* p. 111 and 1373, *ibid.* p. 151 (names uncalendared).

[12] In 1376, *ibid.* p. 241.

[13] *Ibid.* (in 1365), p. 41 and 1369, *ibid.* p. 111. It is perhaps only fair to add that even John Philpot was similarly bound over in 1367 (*ibid.* p. 71) unless the goldsmith of that name is meant, which is not likely as he was only apprenticed in 1379 (Goldsmiths' Wardens Accts. and Court Minutes Bk. A. Pt. i, fo. 55).

[14] *Cal. P. and M.R.* 1381–1412, pp. 58–68. Apart from those mentioned in the Coram Rege Roll the number belonging to the various misteries is as follows ; Tailors 22 ; Goldsmiths 14 ; Armourers 17 ; Skinners, Cutlers

at the re-election of Brembre in October 1384. Perhaps
the most striking feature of these lists is that in the case
of thirteen of the tailors, all the mercers,[1] six of the
armourers and eleven of the goldsmiths,[2] it is by the
masters of their respective misteries that they are brought
before the mayor and aldermen to be bound over " as
persons who speak maliciously of the mayor and aldermen
and of their government "—in the case of the tailors it
is stated that they took part in an assembly in St. Paul's
Church on Election Day and went thence to the Guildhall
to make a disturbance. It is perhaps worthy of remark
that none of Northampton's own mistery, that of the drapers,
appears in the City lists, which means that none of them
continued to create a disturbance after the days actually
following his arrest.[3] It is curious that the tailors, who
numbered so many royal and noble persons among the
honorary members of their fraternity of St. John Baptist,[4]
should have taken such a small part in City affairs at this

and Mercers 3 each; Grocers, Pinners, Brodurers, Fullers, Haberdashers,
Fletchers, Leathersellers and Hatters 1 each. The list in the Coram Rege
Roll is as follows : Mercers 9 ; Drapers 9 ; Goldsmiths 8 ; Cordwainers 5 ;
Saddlers 4 ; Tailors 3 ; Smiths 2 ; Brouderers, Joiners, Bowyers, Hatters,
Leathermongers and Haberdashers 1 each. It will be noticed that there are
no Horners in either list, nor did they, so far as we know, present a petition
to Parliament against Brembre and Exton in 1386. It seems, therefore, somewhat exaggerated to place them " amongst his " (i.e. Northampton's) " most
ardent supporters " as Mr. F. J. Fisher does in his *Worshipful Company
of Horners*, p. 25.

[1] Including John Feraunt, John Chedder, John Vyne and Thomas
Everard.

[2] Adam Bamme is not among them.

[3] None of his mainpernors on his release were drapers—(2 were goldsmiths, one a saddler, one a skinner, one a mercer, one a " broyderer ")
Cal. P.R. 1386, p. 159—All six were drapers when he was bound over on
22 January 1383–84, before his actual insurrection. *Cal. P. and M.R.* 1381–
1412, p. 57.

[4] See Clode, *Memorials of the Merchant Taylors.* It has been suggested
to me by Miss Jeffries Davis that this was because the social aspect of the
fraternity was separate from the business aspect. She compared this case with
the fraternity in Chaucer's Prologue. Thomas Carleton's bequest for a chantry
was left to the Master and Wardens of this fraternity to put into effect—
and he was a " brouder," not a tailor. Northampton's will shows that there
was a fraternity of the drapers in St. Mary le Bow, which may have been of
a similar type to that of the tailors.

time. No tailors became mayor under Richard II and only one, John Redyng, an alderman. Can this account for their championship of Northampton ? It was in their hall and in Goldsmith's Hall that some of Northampton's seditious meetings were held.[1]

That some of these men were brought forward by the heads of their misteries would lead us to expect that they were not prominent persons, and this proves to be the case ; those in the Plea and Memoranda Rolls lists are much more insignificant even than those who were named at Northampton's trial—so much so, indeed, that of scarcely any of them is there any other mention in the City Records.

Northampton's partisans, then, were principally small masters of various non-victualling misteries, notably the mercers, the tailors, the goldsmiths, the drapers, the cordwainers and the armourers, with a sprinkling of men who held a certain amount of real property in the City, and who were just within the ranks of those who held civic office, together with an indefinite, but in all probability large, number of men whose position in the misteries was inferior, or who, perhaps, had no such position at all.[2]

It is not possible [3] to identify his party with the non-victualling misteries as a whole, nor is it possible to think of the struggle as one between greater and lesser misteries as there are to be found members of all the greater non-victualling misteries in the party. All the evidence points to the conclusion that Northampton's secretary, Usk, was speaking the truth when he accused his master of attacking the wealthy and powerful merchants of London by encouraging the jealousies they roused among their poorer fellow-citizens—his object being to maintain himself in power.[4] It is difficult at first sight, however, to explain

[1] See Appendix IV. See also Select Cases before the King's Council (Camden Society), pp. 74-6, for the Petition of the Taylors against Brembre because he had taken away their Charter (1386).

[2] The inquisition printed in Appendix IV, speaks of a band of about 500 men following Northampton in procession down Cheapside the day of his arrest. [3] See above, p. 62, n. 6.

[4] *London English*, pp. 24-5. In saying that " thilk persones that hielden the contrarie of hys menyng were Enemys to alle gode menyng " (*ibid.*) Northampton seems to range himself with all dictators or would be dictators. See also *Peasants' Rising and the Lollards*, p. 29.

how Northampton succeeded in remaining mayor for two years, when Brembre so easily defeated him and his party when they attempted to regain their power on Brembre's election in October 1383. It is true that Northampton was not arrested till nearly four months [1] after he began to conspire against the government of the City, which may have been due to fear, on the part of the capitalists, of the strength of his followers. This, however, would only prove that they under-estimated their own strength—while their inaction may even have been due to contempt and not to fear. To what, then, is this contrast between 1382 and 1383-84 due ? In the first place, in 1382 the king had sent two letters to the City, one to the sheriffs, aldermen and commonalty, and the other to Northampton himself, urging the re-election of the latter as mayor,[2] while the following year royal influence was exerted on Brembre's behalf.[3] Secondly, though in the summer and autumn of 1382 Northampton was inaugurating his campaign against the capitalists, the first steps he took were directed against the monopoly of the London fishmongers, a monopoly which, as its history shows,[4] almost everyone in London, except the monopolists themselves, was eager to attack. According to the continuator of Higden,[5] Northampton lost his popularity when he attempted to interfere with the other London misteries. He does not specify, in any detail, in what directions Northampton interfered, but from the evidence given at his trial we may be sure that it was with the capitalistic element in the misteries.[6]

---

[1] *London English*, pp. 33 ff. (on 7 February).　　[2] *Cal. L.B.H*, p. 200.

[3] *Peasants' Rising and the Lollards*, p. 31, where a serious riot on election day is said to have been prevented by the king's arrival in the City. See also Appendix IV.

[4] See, in particular, the events of 1399, Chapter VII.

[5] Higden, *Polychronicon* IX, p. 29, "cum vellet alias artes eiusdem civitatis super eorum transgressionibus etiam iustificare eorumque pravas consuetudines in melius transmutare et errata corrigere aliquo temptavit emendare . . . inter ipsum maiorem et quasdam artes civitatis predictae gravis dissensionis materia est suborta et percrebuit in tantum quod multi ex eis qui primo fortiter tenuerunt cum eo, amicitiae vinculo procul abiecto, divertentus ab eo noluerunt eius imperio ulterius obedire."

[6] And hence mainly with the greater gilds, in which alone there was this element.

His efforts[1] to control the Common Council by having previous meetings of two men from each of twenty lesser misteries[2] to settle what they would have carried out in the forthcoming council meeting, and his declaration that no one should come to the Common Council from a mistery which opposed him unless chosen by him must have angered considerably the greater misteries, and particularly the wealthier men in them.

The popularity of the attack on the fishmongers throws light on the otherwise very obscure problem why the king should have interfered to secure Northampton's re-election in 1382. Financial reasons would have urged him to oppose, rather than to support, Northampton,[3] while there is no indication that John of Gaunt's [4] influence at court was particularly strong at this time. Probably the feeling in the City against the fishmongers was such that the re-election of Northampton was desired by the majority on account of his known attitude on the subject, and the king's help had been sought because of the opposition which the fishmongers were naturally raising [5] to a policy which was ruining their trade—for Northampton, with the assent of the aldermen and the whole Common Council, had issued certain ordinances in June, forbidding,

[1] Also described in the inquisitions taken at his trial.

[2] Fifteen are named in the inquisition—the Armourers, Girdlers, Loriners, Pinners, Wyrdrawers, Cardmakers, Curreours, Horners, Tilers, Smiths, Dyers, Fullers, Shearmen, Haberdashers, Cordwainers.

[3] Particularly as Brembre had advanced a loan only the month before (*Cal. P.R.* 1381–85, p. 164).

[4] The duke's somewhat mysterious relations with Northampton are discussed below, pp. 81 and 84–5.

[5] The most notorious case of this opposition, however, concerned not a fishmonger but a grocer, Adam Karlill, who in August 1382 " came to the Stokkes where the strangers were selling the fish that they had brought there, according to the ordinances thereon made, and then the said Adam, in a haughty and spiteful manner, cursed the said strangers, saying aloud, in the hearing of all, that he did not care who heard it or knew of it, but that it was a great mockery and badly ordained, that such ribalds as those should be selling their fish within the City " (*Memorials*, pp. 468–9). See also *Cal. P. and M.R.* pp. 21–2, for a case in which a fishmonger struck a woman for talking on Cornhill with a foreigner who had brought fish to sell, and for bringing him water to wash his hands and inviting him to have a drink with her.

among other things, anyone to buy salted fish of merchant strangers to sell again before it had been exposed three days in the open market, or any free fishmonger to enter into partnership with any strange victualler—as the object of such partnerships was to " embrace " fish at the coast.[1] These ordinances were later, in July, explained as meaning that all kinds of fish brought to the City by strangers should be sold by them and their servants, and no one else.[2]

The complaint made against the free fishmongers in Parliament was three-fold[3]—that they kept up the price of fish by refusing to allow anyone to sell it in the City but themselves, that they refused to have any plea[4] touching their mistery settled[5] in any court but their own, and that they used their power of controlling their own mistery to cheat the public by falsifying the baskets in which their fish was sold, in order to increase the weight. Against them, therefore, the ordinances described above had been passed, and the baskets had been burned and the fish in them confiscated, but to make matters sure, a petition on the subject was to be presented in Parliament.[6] Now Parliament was to meet in the first week of October ;[7] the election to the mayoralty was to take place in the second week,[8] when, in all probability, Parliament would still be sitting,[9] so that it was extremely important to ensure the election of a mayor whose opposition to the fishmongers could be counted on. The petition and the statute which came from the petition were far more sweeping than the City ordinances had been. Victuallers were forbidden to hold judicial office in any city or town ; the retail and whole-sale trade in victuals was thrown open to all foreigners, so long as they were not of an enemy nation ; finally, the

---

[1] *Cal. L.B.H*, pp. 191–3.   [2] *Ibid.* p. 194.

[3] *Rot. Parl.* III, pp. 141–2.

[4] " Totes maneres briges et controversies."   [5] " attamez et terminez."

[6] The fishmongers are accused of working against the civic action, *Rot. Parl.* III, p. 142.   [7] *Ibid.* p. 132.

[8] The new mayor was then always elected on 13 October and was sworn and took over his authority on 28 October.

[9] According to Stubbs (*Const. Hist.* I, p. 485). This Parliament sat till 24 October, the date of the general pardon printed at the end of its statutes (*Statutes of the Realm*, II, p. 30).

free fishmongers of London were forbidden altogether to buy fresh fish for re-sale, excepting only eels, pikes and luces.[1] Such a defeat of a great mistery could only have been accomplished by an alliance between those to whom profiteering in food was the most unpardonable of crimes with those who wished to attack the class of great merchants wherever it was vulnerable, and those whose business jealousy was aroused by a mistery that successfully claimed for its " halimot," such an exceptional privilege.[2] In this connection it is significant that when these statutes against the victuallers were repealed during Brembre's mayoralty, it was especially provided that the fishmongers as well as all other victuallers, should " be from henceforth under the governance and rule of the mayor and aldermen . . . as in time past it hath been used."[3] This proves that not even the grocers supported the fishmongers wholeheartedly, and it is worthy of remark that Northampton's second election was supported by all the aldermen, with the exception of Walworth,[4] Brembre, John Brian and William Newport, fishmongers,[5] and John Eston, mercer. Among those who did support it were Philpot, John Hadle and Adam St. Ives, two other prominent grocers, and William More, vintner. It is difficult to believe, indeed, that the opening up of the retail trade in victuals to foreigners affected at all seriously the great merchants of the grocers' and vintners' companies, whose chief business was the import of " spices " and wines in large quantities, and the export of wool and metals and other goods, in lesser

[1] *Rot. Parl.* III, pp. 141–2 (*Statutes of the Realm*, II, pp. 28–9).

[2] See above, p. 14.

[3] *Statutes of the Realm*, II, p. 34. The Statute of 1378, alluded to above, p. 48, permitting merchant strangers to buy and sell victuals and " petites merceries " by wholesale and retail (*Statutes of the Realm*, II, p. 7) was not repealed. The proclamation in the City of December 1383, however, shows that strangers were, in spite of the act, prevented from selling by retail (*Cal. L.B.H*, p. 222).

[4] Who was, of course, a fishmonger. Mr. Postan has called attention in his article on Anglo-Hanseatic Economic Relations (Postan and Power, *English Trade in the 15th Cent.* p. 99) to the decrease in the number of fishmonger aldermen in London, from forty in the fourteenth century to fourteen in the fifteenth.

[5] *Cal. L.B.H*, p. 200.

quantities, in exchange.[1] With the clause forbidding victuallers to hold judicial office in the City it was different. It is probably his attempt to enforce this which is alluded to by Northampton in his petition[2] to the king as being the cause of his downfall, saying that this came about because he put into execution an ordinance made for the common profit of the kingdom and Parliament in the presence of the king. It was repealed, with the rest of the statute of 1382 which related to victuallers in 1383.[3] Nearly all the petitions of the various non-victualling misteries against Exton in the Parliament of 1386 desire its enforcement, the founders[4] even going so far as to declare that victuallers had no right to take part in elections, and that Brembre's second election was invalid on that account alone. In the Merciless Parliament of 1388 it is not the statute of 1382 which is re-enacted, however,[5] but those of 1335 and 1350–51[6] which had, indeed, established free trade in victuals, but made no mention of the prohibition of victuallers holding judicial office.[7] This prohibition was never re-enacted, although that part of the statute which allowed foreigners to sell fish by retail was, in 1399.[8] The reason for this was that Richard had, just before his departure for Ireland, rashly renewed all the privileges of the free fishmongers of London, even restoring their " halimot " with all its past powers.[9]

---

[1] For Brembre's business dealings see above, pp. 4–6 ; Philpot's trade in wine and wool has also been mentioned. He was exporting wool in 1382 as well as in 1380–81 (*Cal. Cl.R.* 1381–85, p. 48), cf. William Venour, also a grocer, and mayor in 1389–90, who was exporting Welsh wool as early as 1369, and as late as 1393 (*Cal. Cl.R.* 1369–74, p. 121 ; *ibid.* 1381–85, p. 283 ; *Cal. P.R.* 1391–96, p. 291). Miss Macaulay gives a particularly interesting account of Venour, among other merchants, in her unprinted thesis, referred to in Chapter I.

[2] *Ancient Petitions*, No. 6417 (See Appendix VI, p. 142).

[3] *Statutes of the Realm*, II, p. 34.   [4] *Ancient Petitions*, 1002.

[5] For the significance of this in relation to the politics of the time, see below.

[6] *Statutes of the Realm*, II, pp. 53–4.

[7] *Ibid.* I, pp. 270 and 315.

[8] *Ibid.* II, p. 118. This was confirmed in 1435 (*ibid.* II, p. 293). In 1392–93 aliens had been forbidden to sell by retail anything but victuals (*ibid.* II, pp. 82–3).   [9] *Cal. L.B.H*, pp. 447–8.

John de Northampton, then, was essentially leader of that party in London which wished to break down the monopoly of power possessed by the merchant capitalists both of the victualling and non-victualling misteries. His party was chiefly composed of small masters, drawn almost entirely from the non-victualling misteries, because Northampton had attacked with great vigour retail victuallers of all kinds,[1] no doubt realising that this was the straightest road to popularity with the mass of Londoners. The great support given him by the goldsmiths can be to a very large extent explained by the exceptional jealousy displayed all through the fourteenth century by the goldsmiths towards the men of other misteries.[2] During the first year of his mayoralty Northampton behaved cautiously, and even secured the support of a large section of the capitalists by his action against the fishmongers. In his second year of office, however, his designs were fully apparent, with the result that he was defeated at the next election.[3] His subsequent conduct disgusted the wealthy Londoners still further, threatening the City, as it did, with riot and disorder. Northampton's first action was to send three of his followers, Richard Norbury, Robert Ryseby and Thomas Usk, to the Duke of Lancaster, to ask him for a royal writ ordering a new election.[4] John of Gaunt refuses:[5] "Nay, certes, writ

---

[1] *Cal. L.B.H*, pp. 183–4.

[2] The " affrays " of 1373 and 1378 have been mentioned above. There had been earlier still a big disturbance between the fishmongers and goldsmiths, in 1339 (*Cal. P. and M.R.* 1323–64, pp. 103–4).

[3] He was later accused of holding a meeting in Goldsmiths' Hall of men of the Common Council to try to prevent Brembre's election by introducing non-electors into the coming meeting. Similar meetings are said to have been held in the church of St. Thomas Acon and the Tailors' Hall. It was also said that John More, the night before the election, in his house in St. Mary-le-bow parish, ordered his servants to come armed to the Guildhall to prevent the election, saying that he and the other sheriff, Simon Wynchecombe would let no one enter who would not vote for Northampton as mayor.

[4] *London English*, p. 28. The details of the narrative of Northampton's behaviour after Brembre's election, unless it is said otherwise, are taken from *C.R.R.* p. 507, partly printed in *Peasants' Rising and the Lollards*, partly in the Appendix IV.

[5] Why Northampton should have hoped for Lancaster's help is still a mystery (see above, p. 77). This is the first record of contact between them that we have (though it is just possible that the acquaintance between them

6

shul ye non have, avise you amonges youre selve."
Northampton also refused to go with the aldermen to
Brembre's house to tell him of his election, as was the City
custom, and had him proclaimed in the City " in the worst
fashion possible." The day after the election he ill-treated
Richard Odiham, the City Chamberlain, so that he stood
in danger of his life on account of his support of Brembre.
On that day also, in spite of the reconciliation, accompanied
by an embrace, which was brought about between the two
rivals by the other aldermen after dinner, in St. Anthony's
Church, he and his followers began conspiracies and
confederacies in St. Paul's Churchyard and St. Michael
Quern, in order to get another election. The appearance
of the king in Cheap quieted matters for a while ; but
after Brembre had been sworn as mayor on 28 October
the unlawful " congregations and conventicles " began
again, by day and night, in the Tailors' Hall, under the
choir of St. Paul's,[1] in the Goldsmiths' Hall in St. John
Zakarie parish, in the parish of St. Mary le Bow[2] and the
churches of the Friars Minor and the Augustinians, their
object being to stir up the people to rebel against Brembre.
Walworth, Philpot, Hadley and other aldermen attempted
again to make peace ; this time Northampton did not even
meet their efforts with politeness. Finally he was summoned
before the King's Council and bound over to keep the
peace.[3] This was on 22 January 1383–84. It seems to have
decided him to use force. He held a big meeting on 26

---

began in 1373 when the former, as Governor of Acquitaine, settled a dispute
between the London drapers and the cloth merchants of Bordeaux (Armitage
Smith, *John of Gaunt*, p. 378 n.). The duke had certainly been at the height
of his unpopularity in London when Parliament met in the first few weeks
of Northampton's first year of office—never, at least, were the Londoners
at less pains to disguise their dislike. The gates of London were kept shut
because of the armed men whom John of Gaunt had brought with him to
Parliament, while the Londoners marked their support of Percy in the quarrel
which then existed between him and the duke, by making the former a freeman of their City (Higden, ix, p. 10)—an action which is all the more remark-
able because of Percy's past attempts to extend his jurisdiction as Marshal over
London.

[1] " In loco qui vocatur le Croudes."   [2] Northampton's own parish.
    [3] Under penalty of forfeiting £5000 to the King (*Cal. P. and M.R.* 1381–
1412, p. 57).

January, and afterwards told Walworth that it would have
been lawful for him to have assembled 8000 men more than
he had done. Then he sent out a summons to about 500
men of the gilds to come to a meeting in Bow Church on
Sunday, 7 February, under pain of a fine of 6s. 8d. each,
if they absented themselves. After they had assembled,
he led them through West Cheap, and as they were passing
outside Ludgate and towards Fleet Bridge, news of the
event was brought to Brembre at Sir Richard Waldegrave's
in St. Michael Hoggenlane where he was at dinner with
Walworth, Philpot, Adam Bamme and other aldermen.
He and Philpot and Vanner and two other men hurried
after Northampton ; seeing him approaching St. Michael
Quern he sent his servant to tell him to stop—the servant
found them in St. Paul's Churchyard ; they refused to stop ;
he demanded three times that they should do so, and on the
third occasion they obeyed and waited for Brembre, lined
up each side of Fleet Bridge. Later the mayor attempted
to persuade Northampton and his followers to go with him,
away from the Carmelite Church, and on his refusal arrested
him and his brother.[1] For the next few days there were
riots and disturbances, John Bere, haberdasher, in Bread
Street even going so far as to compare Northampton with
St. Thomas of Canterbury ; these culminated on Thursday,
11 February, in the shutting of all shops in West Cheap
and Budge Row. It was on the same day that John
Constantyn was executed in Cheap for attempting to raise
an insurrection.[2] The mayor and aldermen probably
wished to make an example of him, to shock the City into
order. They seem to have been successful, at any rate
for the time. Northampton[3] was tried before the King's
Council at Reading in August 1384 and sent as a prisoner
to Tintagel.[4] At the trial he protested against judgment
being passed on him in the absence of his Lord the Duke
of Lancaster.[5] It was not, however, till the spring of 1386

---

[1] This second arrest appears only to have been temporary, as Robert
Comberton later attempted to break down the doors of Brembre's house to
rescue his brother.   [2] *Cal. L.B.H*, p. 231. Probably West Cheap.
[3] With More and Norbury—Essex had fled.
[4] *Cal. Cl. R.*.1384, p. 485.   [5] *Hist. Anglic.* II, p. 116. Higden, IX, p. 46.

that John of Gaunt obtained a lightening of the ex-mayor's sentence—a matter over which the opposition of the City forced him to compromise.[1] Finally, on his return from Spain four years later, the duke obtained full pardon and restitution, not only for Northampton himself, but for his supporters, More and Norbury as well.[2] What is the meaning of all this ? There is certainly sufficient evidence that Northampton was a protégé of John of Gaunt's but none that he was his partisan.[3] The duke must certainly have seen some reason for his efforts on his behalf, but there is no record of any service done him by Northampton or his followers, nor do the chroniclers attempt to account for Lancaster's action. In all probability he had once hoped, through Northampton, to secure a party favourable to himself in London, but his action in the matter of the writ shows either that he was not prepared to interfere openly in London politics or that he could not count on obtaining the writ, and therefore preferred to refuse to attempt to do so. This alternative is supported by the king's subsequent relations with Brembre [4] and by the fact that in 1384 and 1385 Richard showed himself, on more than one occasion, very hostile to his uncle.[5] The duke must have realised before he left for Spain in July 1385,[6] that the opposition to Northampton in London was too strong for the ex-mayor to be an ally of any value ; at any rate he accepted a compromise on the matter of the pardon which conceded more to the Londoners than it did to him.[7]

[1] Higden, IX, pp. 74–5. See the correspondence between John of Gaunt, Brembre and other aldermen, fully calendared, pp. 109–13, in *Cal. P. and M.R.* 1381–1412. See also *Cal. L.B.H*, pp. 279–82 and 307. For the somewhat insolent letter from the City authorities to Lord Zouch on the same subject see below, p. 88, and Appendix V.

[2] *Cal. L.B.H*, p. 359; *Cal. P.R.* 1388–92, pp. 311 and 296–7. Higden, IX, p. 238. (Certain lords and the Commons in Parliament, were also supporting Northampton at this time.)

[3] As some modern writers have asserted.

[4] See Chapter VI.

[5] *Hist. Anglic.* II, pp. 112–6, 126, 131–2 ; *Chron. Ang.* pp. 359–60, 364; Higden, IX, pp. 33, 55–8.

[6] Knighton, II, p. 207.

[7] The duke had asked that Northampton, More and Norbury should be allowed within 40 miles of the City instead of 100 ; the distance was fixed at 80 miles.

That Northampton accompanied him to Spain is unlikely;[1] the unconquered opposition of the Londoners to his pardon may have been one reason why the duke continued to support him when he returned to England—it could not have pleased his pride that the City had successfully run counter to his express wishes.[2] It is unlikely, however, that he continued to be concerned, politically, in Northampton's fate later than the summer of 1386, when his interest in English matters was almost completely eclipsed by his absorption in the affairs of Spain, and, later on, of Aquitaine. But who can tell what influence Northampton's defeat at the election of October 1383 may not have had on his plans ? The party which should have been a check on the capitalists in their own City had been defeated, and yet John of Gaunt made no effort to turn that defeat into a victory or to conciliate the dominant party, in spite of his experience of the support which these capitalists could give, if they chose, to a king who already resented any attempt on the part of his uncle to interfere with the government.[3] The explanation of this may very well be that the duke thought it useless to attempt either resistance or conciliation, and it may be also that the prospect of renewing the struggle with the wealthy merchants, if he continued to take a part in home politics, was a weighty inducement to transfer his energies to affairs overseas.[4]

[1] John of Gaunt declared in his second letter that such was Northampton's intention (*Cal. P. and M.R.* 1381–1412, pp. 110–11) but the fact that in April 1387 efforts were being made to secure his full pardon (*Cal. L.B.H*, pp. 305–7) and again in February 1387–88 (*Rot. Parl.* iii, pp. 248) makes it improbable, as the only evidence that he did so is in a fifteenth-century chronicle (Harl. 565, p. 77) which says that he did so " for doughte elles he myghte have be sclayn whiles he hadde ben oughte of the reaume."

[2] Although Northampton obtained a full pardon in December 1391, he did not regain the City franchise till January 1394–95 (*Cal. L.B.H*, pp. 370 and 419–20). The same is true of More and Norbury.

[3] Cf. his anger when Northampton at his trial expressed his hope that the king would not proceed to judgment in Lancaster's absence (Higden, ix, p. 46).

[4] Miss M. V. Clarke considered that an important link between John of Northampton and John of Gaunt was the opposition of de la Pole, when in alliance with Gaunt, to the Middleburgh Staple, which was undoubtedly favoured by Brembre and others of the group attacked by Northampton (*Fourteenth Century Studies*, pp. 39, ff.), see also A. Steel (*Richard II*, pp. 103 ff.) for another discussion of this point.

CHAPTER VI

THE MERCILESS PARLIAMENT AND LONDON

WHEN at last Northampton did return to the City and to the franchise, though never to take any further part in politics, it was to find the survival of nothing at which he had aimed except the abolition of the fishmongers' monopoly, for the government of the City had become more oligarchic than ever, and he was to live to see it become even more so.[1] He, at any rate, however, was to die a natural death, while his great enemy Brembre had, more than two years before Northampton's return, suffered on the scaffold, on a charge of treason. His ruin was due to his connection with the king, not to his policy in London ; with de Vere, de la Pole, Tresilian and the Archbishop of York he had enjoyed Richard's confidence and aided him in his efforts to establish an independent government, and with them he fell. It is true that some of his actions in London proved a convenient addition to the general charges on which he was appealed of treason, and popular resentment at them probably made it hopeless for his fellow aldermen to attempt his defence, even if they would have dared to take such a course in any case. But the Lords Appellant were in no sense the avengers of Northampton. It is true that retail trade was once more freed, but that great triumph of Northampton—the exclusion of victuallers from office—was not re-established,[2] nor did the Lords

---

[1] Aldermen had been eligible for re-election without any interval since 1384 and in 1394 became irremovable except for " just and reasonable cause," while in 1397 the power of the wards was restrained to the presentment of two men from whom the mayor and aldermen should choose one. The " Jubile " book of ordinances, which was probably directed chiefly against retail victuallers, had been burned in 1387 (*Cal. L.B.H*, p. 303). Election of Common Councillors had returned to the wards in 1384. In 1389 an ordinance had been passed giving the choice of ward representatives to the mayor, who must make his selection in presence of twelve aldermen at least (this, however, may never have become an established practice ; there is at least no record of any Common Council chosen in this manner). (For reference see Chapter III.) [2] *Rot. Parl.* III, p. 247.

restore the compulsory interval of a year before the re-election of any alderman, or the election of the Common Council by misteries.[1] Northampton is only mentioned in one account[2] of Brembre's trial and execution, and even here it is not suggested that Brembre was being punished for his treatment of him ; the attack on Usk, Northampton's secretary, who had turned informer against his employer, is accounted for by his position as under-sheriff of Middlesex, which he held by favour of the king,[3] in order, so it was said, to procure false judgments in that county. Further, Northampton, More and Norbury were expressly excluded from the general pardon issued to all Londoners (except those accused in the Merciless Parliament itself) guilty of felonies and treasons committed between October 1382 and May 1388 ; this pardon was granted in answer to a petition which had in all probability been brought forward by the friends of Northampton ; it was at any rate suggested that it should be used on behalf of some of his supporters.[4] It is an unsettled question whether the member for South-wark in this Parliament was the ex-mayor or some other John Northampton.[5] If it is the same Northampton, he

[1] This inaction on the part of the Lords Appellant seems to have been due partly to the skill of the mayor and aldermen, partly to their own indifference to purely civic matters.

[2] A very important one, however, that in the chronicle of Thomas Favent (Bod. Misc. MSS. 2963), edited by Miss M. McKesack (*Camden Miscellany*, xiv). See also Howell, *State Trials*, i, pp. 118–9.

[3] *Cal. L.B.H*, pp. 316–7 ; *Rot. Parl.* iii, p. 234. The arrests and indictments referred to in his trial as being procured by Usk cannot be taken to mean those of Northampton and his followers, as Usk's appointment only dated from 1387. According to Higden (ix, p. 169), however, Usk went to his death declaring he had only spoken the truth against Northampton, which does indicate that he himself thought he was being punished for the part he had played in the latter's trial.

[4] *Cal. P. and M.R.* 1381–1412, pp. 136–8. They, however, preferred " to put themselves for good or ill upon the country "—and the jury found them not guilty.

[5] *Returns of Members*, i, p. 233. The writ gives only his bare name, and the names of his sureties, John Ive and Richard Houdy (not in the printed return), supply no clue, beyond that they are not those of any of his known supporters. Southwark would probably have been in sympathy with Northampton as it was the capitalists, and particularly the victuallers, who wished to extend the City's jurisdiction over it.

cannot have attended Parliament, which was being held
at Westminster, as he was still not allowed within 80 miles
of the City, for even if it be true that de Vere had interceded
on his behalf with the king,[1] the pardon never was enrolled.

According to the continuator of Higden,[2] the Lords
Appellant banished from Court the Lord de la Souche
who in April 1387 had been attempting to get a full pardon
for Northampton and his friends and who had, for his
pains, received an insolent letter[3] from the mayor and
aldermen in which they told him that they could no longer
hold him to be a faithful subject of the king if he continued
his suit in favour of Northampton, and hinted plainly that
they considered his action due to bribery, the letter ending
in a wish that the Holy Spirit might give him grace and
good counsel, so that he might come to a better point of
view.[4] No doubt his banishment was unconnected with his
championship of Northampton, but it is an additional,
though indirect, proof of the indifference of the Lords
Appellant to the latter's fate.[5]

To return to Brembre, there were no doubt many who
rejoiced in his fall, particularly the misteries who had
petitioned against him in the Parliament of 1386,[6] and who

[1] Higden, IX, p. 93. The chronicler says himself that it did Northampton
little good—but the whole story is improbable.

[2] *Ibid.* p. 116.

[3] *Cal. L.B.H*, p. 305. The letter is printed in full in Appendix V.

[4] After the letter had been sent it was agreed " by the petition of the
whole Commonalty " that the next time Souche came to London the mayor
and aldermen should send for him and persuade him to cease from urging
the City to be reconciled with Northampton, More and Norbury (*Cal.
L.B.H*, p. 307).

[5] This is assuming that the Lord Souche to whom the letter was addressed
was William, Lord Souche of Haryngworth, not Hugh, Lord Souche of
Ashby. There is no indication in the letter itself or its superscription, but
Souche of Haryngworth had a hospice in St. Andrew Parish, " juxta Lyme-
strete " (*Cal. P. and M.R.* 1364–81, pp. 88 and 228, and see also Stow,
II, p. 294), and there is no mention of one anywhere in the City belonging
to Hugh. It was, however, Hugh of Ashby who appears in 1388 as one of the
honorary members of the Gild of St. John Baptist (Clode, *Memorials of
the Guild of Merchant Tailors*, p. 155). The William mentioned as a member
in 1413 (*ibid.* p. 156) must have been the successor of the one who was
banished in 1388. The Haryngworth Souches had estates in Northamptonshire, not so those of Ashby.

[6] See above, pp. 69 and 80.

probably had hated him ever since their charters had been taken from them (forcibly, in the case of the saddlers) [1] in Brembre's first mayoralty of 1377–78. [2] If these petitions are to be believed, Brembre must have shown himself a monster of cruelty, injustice and violence in the two years during which he was mayor after Northampton's fall, but probably they grossly exaggerate. There seems to be little doubt, however, that he used force to secure his re-election in October 1384, probably justifying himself with the thought that he was thereby establishing security in an unquiet City, for Northampton's party still remained active there. [3] Nor does he seem to have been above taking a personal revenge, at any rate he must have had the reputation that he was not—witness the complaint of Joan, wife of John Payn, goldsmith, one of Northampton's supporters, who herself had come outside Brembre's house while he held Northampton a prisoner there and did all she could to excite the mob to break into the house and release him. In 1386 she was in Ludgate at the suit of Brembre, and was ill-treated by the keeper of the prison who " desiring to please the said Sir Nicholas procured and abetted the prisoners there to beat her in her bed and else where so continually and so horribly that her life scarce endured." [4] With regard to the judicial murders that he is supposed to have committed as mayor, it is difficult to see what object he could have had in the execution of twenty-one people, chaplains and others, imprisoned in Newgate under charges of felony. [5] If, however, the " Foul Oke," where these executions are said to have taken place, was at

---

[1] See their petition.   [2] *Cal. L.B.H*, p. 193.

[3] Not all of those who created disturbances did so from reasoned motives, some seem to have loved conflict for its own sake—e.g. " William Wodecok, tailor, who came to the Guildhall on election day, contrary to the proclamation, and went thence to his shop and fetched a sword, buckler and poleaxe, *hoping* that a riot would arise ! " (*Cal. P. and M.R.* 1381–1412, p. 67), (the italics are mine).

[4] *Cal. P. and M.R.* 1381–1412, p. 157. This even was not the end of her sufferings, but as a result of her plea the keeper of the prison paid her 20s. damages. It is more difficult to discover the rights and wrongs of a case which a debtor of his brought into Chancery (*Select Cases in Chancery*, Selden Soc. pp. 8–9).

[5] *Rot. Parl.* III, pp. 231 ; *Camden Miscellany*, XIV, p. 5.

Hatcham,[1] it was little more than a mile from Brembre's manor of Lewisham,[2] which is, to say the least, an interesting coincidence.

It was not for such actions, however, that Brembre lost his life in 1388 ; for the past four years and more [3] he had steadily supported Richard II, and now he paid for that support.[4] His loan to the Crown of £1333 6s. 8d. in September 1382 [5] foreshadowed a period of close financial co-operation between the City and the government, which can be compared with the first three years of Richard's reign ; this period may be said actually to begin in September 1383, when the City advanced £2666 13s. 4d.[6] No doubt there is a connection between this loan and the granting of a full " Inspeximus " Charter in November,[7] and the support given to Brembre in his difficulties with Northampton mentioned above [8] and at his second election.[9] The next series of loans was caused by the renewal of the French war in May 1385 ; the City advanced £5000 in June [10] and Brembre himself £666 13s. 4d. some time before March in the next year.[11] £1000 was also lent by the City in October 1385 " to provide men at arms and archers for the relief of Ghent," [12] and £4000 in November 1386,[13] the French having attempted an invasion on the south coast not long before. Exton had by this time succeeded Brembre as mayor, and the latter began to take a more active part

---

[1] As Prof. Skeat considers (see R. F. G. Kirk, *Chaucer's Life Records*, Part IV, pp. xl–xli).

[2] And only about three from his manor of Greenwich.

[3] From October 1383 to October 1386 of this period he had himself been mayor. He was then succeeded by Nicholas Exton, fishmonger, who was re-elected in October 1387. Brembre was appealed of treason the next month.

[4] Mr. Steel, *E.H.R.* October 1936, p. 592, has shown that Brembre received £2166 worth of bad tallies from the Crown, so that his financial reward was not very satisfactory either.

[5] *Cal. P. R.* 1383–85, p. 164.   [6] *Ibid.* p. 307, see above, p. 7.

[7] *Cal. C.R.*, 1341–1417, p. 294.

[8] pp. 82 ff. and *Cal. L.B.H*, p. 231.

[9] *Ibid.* pp. 250–1 ; Higden, IX, p. 68.

[10] *Cal. L.B.H*, p. 267.   [11] *Cal. P.R.* 1385–89, p. 121.

[12] I am indebted for this information to Mr. Mead, who mentions it in his unprinted thesis.

[13] *Cal. P.R.* 1385–89, p. 240 ; *Cal. L.B.H*, pp. 293–4.

in general politics. He was a member [1] of the famous Council held at Nottingham in August 1387 when the questions were put to the justices as to the legality of the appointment of the Council of eleven in the previous November ; he became closely connected with de la Pole,[2] and he seems to have been an intermediary between the City and Richard II.[3] When the crisis came, however, not all Brembre's efforts could raise the City against the Lords Appellant (though a proclamation is said to have been made in London, when Arundel's army lay outside the walls, forbidding anyone to sell it arms or victuals and commanding its members to be treated as rebels).[4] There is no such proclamation, however, in the Letter Book,[5] the City, indeed, seems to have acted with caution from the very first. When the mayor and aldermen were summoned to Windsor by the king,[6] almost immediately after the lords had " appealed " Brembre, de Vere, the Archbishop of York, de la Pole and Tresilian, in the hope that an armed force could be raised in the City, they answered discouragingly, but evasively [7]—the Londoners never burned their boats until they were quite sure which was the winning side—putting forward the excuse that as craftsmen and merchants they were unskilled in war. Later, this action of theirs was described by the lords as a refusal to countenance a plot to murder them by treachery.[8] Froissart, indeed, is the only chronicler who implies that they had

---

[1] Knighton, II, p. 236.   [2] *Chron. Ang.* p. 373.

[3] *Cal. L.B.H,* p. 315.

[4] *Camden Misc.* XIV, Thomas Favent's *Chronicle,* pp. 5–12. The mayor and aldermen are here said to have gone with the King and Brembre and the four others who were about to be appealed, to the shrine of St. Edward the Confessor on 10 November.

[5] The Letter Book is always noticeably reticent on general political questions, compare its silence at the time of the " Good " Parliament, at that of the taking of the City into the king's hand, and at that of the deposition of Richard II. This was probably due to caution. In the last case some folios have been torn out. Two accounts of what happened in London are, however, very full—that in Higden and that in Favent.

As the former was probably written by a Westminster monk and the latter probably by an eye-witness in the Parliament, they are of considerable value.

[6] *Cal. L.B.H,* p. 321.   [7] Higden, IX, pp. 108–9.

[8] *Rot. Parl.* III, p. 231.

so refused.[1] Only a month before, the mayor, aldermen and commonalty[2] had taken an oath of allegiance[3] to Richard " against all those who are or shall become rebels to his person or royalty." It is interesting to note that in the City version of this oath a clause renouncing the " evil opinions " of Northampton and his accomplices was inserted, but it was omitted in the copy sent to the king.[4] In spite of this oath, and in spite of Brembre's influence,[5] exercised at the time when the lords lay at Clerkenwell, the mayor and aldermen allowed their army to enter London as soon as its leaders demanded admittance for it. The continuator of Knighton tells us that the lords had previously sent a letter to them bidding them not to aid the appealed " as you wish . . . the safety of your said city."[6] This chronicler represents Exton as willing to support Richard, but unable to do so on account of the attitude of the Londoners.[7] Walsingham declares that the Londoners admitted the lords for fear that the mob would do so if they refused, and then proceed to loot the houses of the rich.[8] The writer of the *Chronicon Angliae* attributes the greatness of the numbers of those who flocked to the standards of the lords to the fact that they hoped to share in a sack of London ;[9] finally, the continuator of Higden speaks of the offer made by the lords themselves to mediate between the crafts of London,[10] an offer which the Londoners politely refused, but which

---

[1] Froissart (Berners edn.), III, pp. 465 ff., 487 ff.

[2] Probably here meaning the Common Council.

[3] *Cal. L.B.H*, pp. 314-15. The procuring of this oath (but with no mention of Northampton or his followers) was later one of the points of accusation against Brembre (*Rot. Parl.* III, p. 235). Th. Favent seems to twist this incident into an effort to get the Londoners to agree that when summoned by Brembre they would be " disobedient and contrary to the King and the royal power," p. 5 (*Camden Misc.* XIV).

[4] *Cal. L.B.H*, p. 315. Dr. Sharpe in his introduction to this Letter Book (p. xliv) calls attention to this fact.

[5] Th. Favent's *Chronicle*, p. 12.   [6] Knighton, II, p. 246.

[7] *Ibid.* p. 244. For Exton's difficult position see below, p. 94.

[8] Walsingham, II, p. 171 " Quia nisi maiores Dominis aperirent, communes civitatis et pauperes, qui plus affectabant seditionem quam pacem, paraverunt se ad introducendum Dominos, cum plebe sua, et diripiendum quicquid erat in domibus divitium pretiosium."

[9] *Chron. Angl.* p. 387.   [10] Higden, IX, pp. 117-18.

must have secretly filled those in authority with dismay
and confirmed them in their determination to conciliate
as far as possible those who had made such an offer. Their
opportunity came to do so with the trial of Brembre which
began on 17 February 1387–88. He was the only one of
the five who had been appealed who had not fled, though
his trial was to be interrupted by the discovery of Tresilian
in hiding.[1] He had pleaded " Not Guilty " to all the
charges against him.[2] These were principally as follows :
first, of having agreed with and supported Archbishop
Neville, de Vere and de la Pole in their alleged policy of
alienating the king from his subjects and particularly from
the great lords,[3] and of taking to themselves " Roial Poar
Seigneurie et Sovereinite " over the King's person ;
secondly, of having used his position at Court to make his
own fortune [4] by gifts of land and jewels and issues from
the taxes, and of having procured lands and offices for
relatives and those who would give him a commission on
the grant ; thirdly, of having attempted to raise London
in arms [5] to defeat the aims of the Lords Appellant and to
put them to death, and of having abetted the efforts which
the rest of the accused were making in other parts of the
country, and particularly in Wales and Chester, with the
same object ; [6] of having procured the answers unfavourable
to the lords from the justices at the council at Nottingham ;[7]
finally, of having acted unjustly in his judicial capacity.[8]
He claimed trial by battle, but it was refused by his judges,
who declared that they would decide on evidence taken
" by all essential necessary, reliable and suitable means." [9]
How they obtained evidence is not stated in the Roll,
which simply declares that they pronounced him guilty

---

[1] Favent's *Chronicle*, p. 17.
[2] *Rot. Parl.* III, p. 238.
[3] *Ibid.* III, pp. 230 and 232.
[4] *Ibid.* p. 230.
[5] *Ibid.* pp. 231 and 235.
[6] *Ibid.* p. 232.
[7] *Ibid.* pp. 232-3.
[8] *Ibid.* p. 231. Not only by the judicial murders mentioned above but
by causing delays and taking bribes and obtaining Charters of pardon for
people guilty " de horribles felonies et tresons." He was not, however, accused
of trying to buy help against the Appellants from the King of France by the
surrender of Calais, as the Archbishop, de Vere and de la Pole were.
[9] *Rot. Parl.* III, p. 238.

on it, the trial having lasted four days. The continuator of
Higden, however, supplies further details.[1] The king, so he
says, defended Brembre, though without success. His case
was then examined by the Duke of York, the earls of Kent,
Salisbury and Northumberland and eight other great lords,
who found him Not Guilty. Next, two members of every
London mistery were summoned to give evidence, but with
no result. Finally, Brembre was condemned on the opinion
of the mayor, aldermen and recorder of London, who,
when asked whether they thought he had been cognisant
of these treasonable matters, replied that they thought
he was more likely to have known of them than not, the
recorder adding, on being questioned, that if he did know
of them and concealed his knowledge, he was worthy of
death. It may be remarked that the cutlers,[2] in their
petition to the Parliament of 1386, asked that this recorder,
William Cheyne,[3] together with one of the aldermen,
Hugh Fastolf, who was also sheriff, should be ousted from
office for ever, because they were accomplices of Brembre's.
The mayor, Nicholas Exton, fishmonger, was in a particularly
difficult position. It is clear by the petitions of the crafts
in 1386 that his downfall was sought by them as eagerly
as the downfall of Brembre.[4] Though Brembre had been
the man who had actually supplanted Northampton in
office and effected his arrest, it was Exton who had been
notorious, both in the City[5] and in Parliament[6] as the
champion of the free fishmongers, a member of whose
gild he was himself, and it was he who had been deprived

---

[1] Higden, IX, pp. 166–8. This part of the Chronicle is in Latin, but the
part immediately before, which gives the articles of the appeal is in French,
and follows the printed roll very closely, though not exactly.

[2] F. Welch, *History of the Cutler's Coy.* I, p. 266.

[3] Cheyne was Recorder from 1376 (at least) to 1389, and probably later
(*Cal. L.B.H*, pp. 50, 348, 395).

[4] See, for example, that of the Mercers, *Rot. Parl.* III, p. 225. It is curious
that the burning of the " Jubile Book," which is one of the main complaints
of the crafts against Exton, did not take place, according to Letter Book H,
until 1387, the year after the petitions (*Cal. L.B.H*, p. 303). It had been
revised in 1384 by a committee of 43 on which neither Brembre nor Exton
sat, though W. Walworth, A. Bamme, Sibil, Tonge and Karlille did
(*ibid.* pp. 234–5).

[5] *Cal. L.B.H*, pp. 203–5.　　　　　　[6] *Rot. Parl.* III, p. 243.

of his office of alderman for his opposition to Northampton as mayor in August 1382,[1] and who had been forced to leave the City for the time.[2] It appears that he expected to be attacked at the same time as Brembre, for he asked permission to resign his office of mayor, a petition which the king refused,[3] probably hoping to secure the support of London against the lords by keeping Exton in power. If this indeed were the case Richard's hopes were greatly disappointed. Apart from the fact that Thomas of Wood-stock still probably bore a personal grudge against Brembre,[4] the latter stood in their eyes, as did Michael de la Pole,[5] for the interference with matters of state on the part of merchant capitalists, and the independence of the great land-owners acquired by the Crown through the great sums which these capitalists were willing to advance, resentment against which probably underlay all the attacks of the nobles on the king's servants of this type during this period. It is interest-ing to speculate whether, if Walworth and Philpot had still been alive,[6] they would have been involved in the same ruin as Brembre. It is, on the other hand, even possible that Philpot might have been long-sighted enough and popular enough to have raised London on Richard's behalf.[7] As it was, however, Exton and the aldermen saved the City from any interference in its internal affairs on the part of the lords, by refusing all support to the king, and by deserting Brembre entirely, even when given an opportunity to defend

---

[1] *Cal. L.B.H*, p. 196.

[2] The sentence against him was not reversed till 1384 (*ibid*. pp. 233, 234).

[3] *Cal. L.B.H*, p. 196.   [4] See above, p. 48.

[5] Professor Tout, in his article on Pole in the *D.N.B.*, calls attention to the fact that he is regarded by the chroniclers of the day (who in this reflected the opinion of the great landowners) entirely as " a merchant and the son of a merchant " in spite of his military experience under the Black Prince and John of Gaunt. It seems that Brembre did not think in this way about himself—see, for example, his claim at his trial that he was ready to defend his innocence with his body " come Chivaler deust faire " (*Rot. Parl.* III, p. 238). His point of view about himself would not recommend him in the eyes of the great nobles.

[6] Walworth died either in December 1385 or January 1385–86 (*Cal. Wills*, II, p. 251). Philpot was dead by May 1384 (*Cal. Cl.R.* 1381–85, p. 375).

[7] But compare his inaction at the time of the " Good " Parliament (Chapter II.).

him. Brembre's death was therefore in a certain indirect
sense due to the activities of Northampton's party, because
it was the very existence of this party which made the rulers
of the City conscious that the lords were possessed of not
only an excuse for interference, but also a means of attack
within London itself. That Exton's fear for himself was
not groundless, and that he succeeded in making the lords
willing to protect him, are proved by the record of " a
general rumour in London and the suburbs among the
commons of the City that he had by petition to the prelates,
nobles and magnates of the ' last '[1] Parliament sought
the derogation and annulment of its liberties and that
Robert Knolles might be made captain thereof." [2] On
the petition of Exton the king issued a notification declaring
that he had caused the prelates, nobles and magnates of the
present Parliament to be questioned, who . . . unanimously
protested that he had never pursued any such course.[3]
Exton also considered it worth while to obtain for himself,
in the same month, a pardon for all treasons and felonies,[4]
as had also William Venour,[5] grocer, alderman of Tower,
at that time[6] one of the sheriffs.[7] Exton's connection with

---

[1] i.e. the Merciless Parliament ; the entry is dated 4 October, Cambridge
—where the second Parliament of 1388 was held in September (see *Statutes
of the Realm*, II, p. 55).

[2] *Cal. P.R.* 1385–89, p. 514.

[3] *Ibid.* The Lords Appellant were still in power, as Richard did not
assert his independence till May, 1389 (Walsingham, *Hist. Anglic.* II, p. 181 ;
Cal. Cl.R. 1385–89, p. 671). For the attitude of Northampton's party towards
Exton, see also Higden, IX, p. 179. These letters patent appear in the City
Records (*Cal. L.B.H*, pp. 330–1).

[4] *Cal. P.R.* 1385–89, p. 505. It is curious that though the pardon is dated
1 October, Exton is described as " late mayor " when he only ceased to be
mayor on 13 October (*Cal. L.B.H*, p. 335). Perhaps he thought an additional
protection for when he no longer held office was gained thereby.

[5] *Cal. P.R.* 1385–89, p. 502.

[6] The date of the pardon was 4 August. Venour had been chosen sheriff
by Exton, then mayor, on 21 September 1387, and was therefore approaching the close of his year of office (*Cal. L.B.H*, p. 313).

[7] A rumour was started in the City in August that the other sheriff,
Hugh Fastolf, grocer (the same whom the Cutlers hated), had been arrested
and imprisoned in the Tower by order of the King's Council, together with
John Chircheman, grocer, alderman of Bishopsgate, whose head, it was
asserted, the Duke of Gloucester had broken (*Cal. L.B.H*, pp. 329–30).

the Government, too, though not so marked as that of Brembre, was sufficient to make it likely that the lords would support his enemies unless he made his peace with them. He was Brembre's fellow collector of the wool-subsidy in the Port of London,[1] the king had lately granted him the wardship of certain manors in Kent [2] and he held the constableship of Northampton Castle.[3] This office he exchanged in March 1387–88 for a pension of 6d. a year [4] " with the consent of the Council,"[5] but he retained his possession of the office of collector,[6] William Venour (who had a few years back been the collector of the petty custom in Southampton [7]) becoming his colleague in the place of Brembre. It is not without significance that both these men advanced money to the Government at the time when it was being controlled by the Lords Appellant—Venour £500 some time before May 1388,[8] and Exton, together with the widow of Adam Fraunceys, over £1000 about the same time.[9] (The City itself was to lend £5000 in March.[10]) Henry Vanner, vintner, Brembre's brother-in-law, was also one of the aldermen at the time of Brembre's trial, as was William Venour, to whom, together with Vanner and three other men, Brembre, as has already been said,[11] had transferred all his personal property on 15 October 1387.[12] Apart from these, eleven [13] of the aldermen had sat

---

[1] *Cal. Cl.R.* 1385–89, p. 366.   [2] *Ibid.* p. 350.

[3] *Cal. P.R.* 1385–89, p. 276.   [4] *Ibid.* p. 414.

[5] *Cal. Cl.R.* 1385–89, p. 381.   [6] *Ibid.* p. 398.

[7] *Ibid.* p. 22.   [8] *Cal. P.R.* 1385–89, p. 447.

[9] *Ibid.* p. 478. It is possible, however, that the whole sum was advanced by Agnes Fraunceys and that Exton was only acting as trustee to the estate, being mayor at the time. See Sharpe, *Cal. Wills,* 11, p. 171. Agnes had had business connections with Brembre in 1375 (*H.R.* 103. 183) and in 1387 (*ibid.* 116. 37). In this case she had been among those to whom he had handed over his lands and tenements in September of that year. See also Catalogue of Ancient Deeds (Exchequer T. R. Diplomatic Documents, p. 166), for her share with Brembre and others in a release of a house in King Street, Westminster, which had been John Boterwyk's).

[10] *Cal. P.R.* 1385–89, p. 425. Mr. Mead, in his unprinted thesis, says that the significance of this loan should not be exaggerated. It was short dated, well secured, and the money was—in theory at any rate—to be spent on naval defences and the safe-guarding of the seas.

[11] Above, p. 4.   [12] *Cal. P. and M.R.* 1381–1412, p. 134.

[13] Elys, Staundon, Chircheman, St. Ives, Hende, W. More, Rote, Fraunceis, Organ, Hadley and Welford.

continuously since March 1383–84, three continuously for the
past three years (Exton, Fressh and Shadworth), and only
Twyford and Wotton, A. Bamme and Olyver had not
held office under Brembre and so officially supported his
policy in the City ; [1] even they had acquiesced when a
similar policy was pursued by Exton.[2] The Court of Aldermen, therefore, which deserted Brembre in this fashion
was almost identical with that which had written to John
of Gaunt in 1386 to inform him that the opposition in the
matter of Northampton's pardon of which he was complain-
ing was not due to Brembre alone, but to the Court's
unanimous action,[3] while every alderman present at
Brembre's trial shared the responsibility for the letter sent
to Lord de la Souche expressing a similar point of view.[4]
It is interesting in this connection to compare the tone
adopted by the rulers of the City to these two nobles [5]
with their action when an armed force outside London
made a discontented party within the gates a danger to
be reckoned with and a great lord one whose opinion was
to be deferred to. In 1386 the concession that Northampton
in his banishment should be allowed to approach twenty
miles nearer London was represented as an act of con-
descension on the part of the City, while the duke was
requested not to meddle with London affairs without
first acquiring accurate information from the City authorities
on the subject in question : the letter to Lord de la Souche [6]
in 1387 is couched in a tone of scarcely veiled rudeness,
and it contains a declaration of the City's determination to
stand by Richard II against all his enemies which contrasts
forcibly with the action eventually taken.

[1] Bamme and Olyver had sat since March 1385–86, Twyford and Wotton
since March 1386–87 (see *Cal. L.B.H*, pp. 229–30, 263, 283–4, 304). Of the
aldermen in 1388 seven were grocers, three goldsmiths, three mercers, two
skinners, two vintners and two fishmongers, one wax-chandler and one
woolmonger. There is no return for Cheap (*Cal. L.B.H*, pp. 304–5).

[2] E.g. *Cal. L.B.H*, p. 305.

[3] *Cal. P. and M.R.* 1381–1412, p. 111.

[4] See Appendix V.

[5] John of Gaunt, at the time of this correspondence, was at Plympton in
Devon, busy with his preparations for the expedition to Spain.

[6] See above, p. 88, and Appendix V.

Abandoned by those who had worked with him and supported him, Brembre was hanged on 20 February. Higden says that his penitence moved the onlookers to tears ;[1] Favent describes how Northampton's son demanded of him in his last moments whether his treatment of his father had been just, and declares that Brembre confessed that it had not been so.[2] He himself seems to have been childless ; the name which he made so famous in London for a short period drops out of the City records altogether, except when some echo of his old rivalry with Northampton provides a rallying cry for factious misteries.[3]

The circumstances which attended Brembre's fate suggest almost inevitably the question whether history did not repeat itself eleven years later, that is, whether Henry of Lancaster was not welcomed as king by the Londoners merely because of their fear of his army ? A consideration of the events of these eleven years, and particularly of the " Taking of the City into the King's hand," which took place in 1392,[4] show that this was not so. Nor were the internal politics of London affected at all by the victory of the Lords Appellant over the king. Brembre's ruin was personal : the power of the capitalist party in London remained unshaken. At first sight it might appear as if this were not so, for Exton's successor in October 1388 was the Nicholas Twyford, goldsmith, who had quarrelled with Brembre in 1378 and attempted to succeed him in 1384 ;[5] his election four years later took place after the City had received letters of Privy Seal ordering it " to secure the peaceable election of a trusty and loyal Mayor." [6] Twyford, however, though twelve years before he had supported annual election of aldermen and the election to the Common

---

[1] Higden, ix, pp. 168–9.

[2] Favent, p. 18. This is the version which appears in Howell's *State Trials*.

[3] A proclamation was made as late as 1396–97, that no one should speak or give his opinion as to either Brembre or Northampton because this led to dissension (*Cal. L.B.H*, p. 364, and *Memorials*, pp. 526–7), Adam Bamme was then mayor. There are indications, in the references to his confiscated property and elsewhere, that his widow, Idonia, did not lose her own inheritance from her father, John Stodeye.

[4] *Cal. L.B.H*, pp. 377–81. See below, Chapter VII.

[5] See above, pp. 68–9.   [6] *Cal. L.B.H*, pp. 334–5.

Council by misteries,[1] had by now certainly thrown in his lot with the oligarchic party, as his ordinance of January 1388–89 shows.[2] The other ordinance passed at the same meeting of the Court of Aldermen—that no one should be mayor for more than one year at a time, but that he might be re-elected after a term of five years—is indicative of the desire of the aldermanic class that the office of mayor should not be confined to one or two members of that class, but it is indicative of nothing more. The conflicts which the continuator of Higden reports as taking place at elections to the mayoralty[3] were, on the part of the candidates, caused by personal rivalry which used craft feeling to secure its ends. Election of one rather than another does not mean a change of policy as in the case of Northampton and Brembre. It cannot be maintained, either, that this ordinance of January 1388–89 was inspired by craft feeling; if the records for the twenty-three years following the ordinance are examined, it will be seen that seventeen individuals held the office of mayor, representing seven misteries,[4] while in the twenty-three years before, fifteen individuals had been mayor, representing six misteries.[5] It was probably the practice of the seven years preceding 1388–89 which was the direct cause of the ordinance; in that period there had been only three mayors—but each of these mayors was representative of a different mistery.[6] It is significant, however, of the jealousy felt by the other misteries against the free fishmongers, that whereas in the twenty-three years before 1388 the fishmongers had seven times been represented in the office of mayor, in the twenty-three years following it they were represented but once; this one fishmonger mayor, William Askham, was the successor in business of Walworth, who had

---

[1] *Cal. L.B.H*, p. 38.

[2] *Ibid.* p. 347. This ordinance gave the choice of the common councillors to the mayor, who was to select a fixed proportion of representatives from each ward in the presence of twelve aldermen at least.

[3] Higden, IX, pp. 51 and 217.

[4] The goldsmiths, fishmongers, grocers, drapers, mercers, vintners and ironmongers (there is only one of these last).

[5] The goldsmiths, fishmongers, grocers, drapers, mercers and skinners. The similarity of the misteries represented is worthy of remark.

[6] Northampton was a draper, Brembre a grocer, and Exton a fishmonger.

twice been mayor, and was himself the apprentice of John
Lovekyn, twice mayor in this period of twenty-three years,
and twice before 1365.[1] That the jealousy was felt by the
misteries against the fishmongers and not against the
" victuallers " in general is clear, for while there were seven
grocer mayors between 1365 and 1388, there was only
one less between 1388 and 1410, while there was a vintner
mayor in the latter period, and none in the former.[2]

At the close of Richard II's reign, therefore, the governing body of the City was still, as it had been at its beginning,
composed of members of the merchant capitalist class,
stronger, it would seem, than ever, for it had succeeded in
distributing more equally the balance of power within
itself by abolishing the extraordinary privileges of the
free fishmongers.[3] The conflict with the class of small
masters who had wished to break its monopoly had come
and gone, and it was so secure that it could afford to allow
the return of the leaders of this opposing party to citizenship.

The rulers of London were, therefore, in a position to
render great assistance to Richard against Henry of
Lancaster if they chose. Why did they not so choose ?

[1] Harl. 565, ed. Nicholas, pp. 88–9. *Cal. Wills*, II, p. 118. Beaven, I, 55.
The chronicler adds that they were " alle schireves and meires ech after other
in on house."

[2] For the mayors of this period see *Calendars of Letter Books G, H and I*,
passim, and Stow's Survey (ed. Kingsford), II, pp. 167–71.

[3] For the restoration of these privileges in 1399 see the next chapter.

CHAPTER VII

THE "TAKING OF THE CITY INTO THE KING'S HAND," AND THE COMING OF HENRY OF LANCASTER

THE process known as the "Taking of the City into the King's hand," involved the deposition of the elected officers of the City, the appointment of a warden, usually not a London citizen, in the place of the mayor, royal nomination of sheriffs, and the suspension of all the privileges of the City. This measure was very frequently resorted to by the Crown in the thirteenth century—from 1265–70, for example, because of the support which the City had given to de Montfort; [1] and again from 1285–98 because of its resistance to the great " Iter " of 1285. [2] Under Edward II, during the " Iter " of 1321 London was again " Taken into the King's hand," [3] but its liberties were soon restored in the hope of securing its support against the barons. Edward III, in his first charter to the City, [4] granted that this method of punishment should not be employed because of the misconduct of individuals, or even of individual officials of the City. [5] The whole question was further clarified by

[1] *London and the Kingdom*, I, p. 99.   [2] *Ibid.* p. 122.

[3] *Ibid.* p. 146. London was at this time finding difficulty in getting the king to repay its loans (Mead, unprinted thesis), a situation which repeated itself in these last few years of Richard II's reign.

[4] Miss Davis says in her article on the sources for this Eyre—(*Bull. of Hist. Research*, VII, (1929–30))—that " the first charter of Edward III gave the citizens all and more than all that they had claimed before the justices at the Eyre." Similarly the taking of the City into the king's hand in 1392 was followed seven years later by concessions from a successor who had realised the danger of antagonising the City. See below, p. 111.

[5] *Liber Albus*, I, p. 147. " Quod libertas civitatis Londoniarum non capiatur in manum Domini Regis pro aliqua personali transgressione vel iudicio personali alicuius ministri eiusdem civitatis ; nec quod Custos in eadem ea occasione deputetur."

the statute of 1354[1] which stated that because the citizens
of London have no remedy against misgovernment on the
part of their own officials, if the mayor, sheriffs and aldermen do not " cause to be redressed " " the errors, defaults
and misprisions which be notoriously used in the City,"
they shall, for the first offence be fined 1000 marks, for the
second 2000 marks, and for the third " the Franchise and
Liberty of the City " shall " be taken into the King's hand."
The evidence as to the guilt of the City officials was to be
held by means of inquests, at the Michaelmas following,
not of Londoners, but of men of Kent, Essex, Sussex, Hert-
ford, Buckingham and Berks,[2] " before the King's Justices
which shall be to the same assigned." [3] In accordance with
the Charter of 1327, though twice in Edward III's reign
the mayor was deposed by order of the king,[4] in both cases
his successor was elected by the citizens, and no warden
was appointed, no liberties were suspended. When, therefore, in June 1392, Richard II discharged the mayor[5] and
sheriffs[6] from their offices and committed them to prison,
appointing Sir Edward Dalyngrigge, warden of the City,[7]
and two Londoners to be sheriffs,[8] he was reviving a practice
of which the City had had no experience for seventy years.
Nor was the procedure laid down by the statute of 1354

[1] *Statutes of the Realm*, i, pp. 346–7. The ordinance was to extend " to
all Cities and Boroughs of the Realm where such Defaults or Misprisions
be used and not duly corrected nor redressed " (*ibid.* p. 347). There is no
mention of this statute in the Calendar of Letters Book G or H, or in their
introductions.

[2] The locality of the jurors was to vary according to the locality of the
City or borough involved.

[3] Later it says, " And because the Sheriffs of London be parties to this
business, the Constable of the Tower and his Lieutenant shall serve in the
place of the Sheriffs to receive the writs."

[4] Adam de Bury was deposed in January 1365–66 (*Cal. L.B.G*, p. 205)
and Adam Stable in March 1376–77 (*Cal. L.B.H*, p. 60). For the latter
incident see above, p. 24.

[5] John Hende, draper.

[6] John Shadeworth, mercer, and Henry Vanner, vintner.

[7] *Cal. L.B.H*, p. 379; *Cal. P.R.* 1391–96, p. 100. Dalyngrigge was
replaced as warden by Sir Baldwin Radyngton at the end of July (*ibid.*
p. 125) because, according to Walsingham, the former had sworn to the citizens
that he would defend their customs (*Hist. Ang.* ii, p. 209).

[8] I.e. Gilbert Maghfeld, ironmonger, and Thomas Newtone, mercer.

altogether followed, as there is no indication that the discharge was for a third offence. Such a commission, however, as was provided for in the statute, was set up, including among its members the Dukes of York and Gloucester, but we have no record of its proceedings, and only know that it found the mayor, sheriffs and aldermen guilty, and therefore liable to the fine of 3000 marks.[1] The price of the recovery of the liberties of the City was first set at £100,000, but in September this was lowered to £10,000, while the fine of 3000 marks was excused altogether.[2] That money was the king's object seems indisputable ; the fact that the arrest and deposition of the mayor and sheriffs and the appointment of the warden took place three days before the commission of enquiry was set up[3] shows that the " misgovernment " of the City was only a pretext. It is also recorded that in the previous February an attempt had been made to raise money in another fashion, by a distraint of knighthood in the City ;[4] the last attempt of this kind had been made in 1365–66[5] and also proved a failure.[6] According to most contemporary chroniclers[7] the king had recently attempted to raise a loan in London, and, having failed to do so, punished the citizens by removing the Courts of Justice to York[8] and by taking the City into his hand.[9] Pretexts for the king's action were found in

[1] *Cal. P.R.* 1391–96, pp. 130 and 166.

[2] *Ibid.* pp. 130 and 226.

[3] *Ibid.* p. 166 ; *Cal. L.B.H*, pp. 377–9.

[4] *Ibid.* p. 378.   [5] *Cal. L.B.G*, p. 205.

[6] *Cal. L.B.H*, p. 378, n. 1. The return referred to in this note was that no one " had £40 a year in land or rents for certain, in as much as tenements in the City were let sometimes for more and sometimes for less and frequently stood empty and were not let, and were often in want of repair. For these reasons, and because of fires and other dangers arising to houses no certain value of them could be ascertained " (*Cal. L.B.F*, p. 105).

[7] Walsingham, *Hist. Ang.* II, pp. 207–10 ; Higden, IX, p. 270 ; *Eulog. Hist. III*, pp. 367–8.

[8] *Cal. L.B.H*, p. 378. This migration of the Courts to York is held by Miss D. M. Broome, in her essay on " Exchequer Migrations to York " (in " Essays in Mediaeval History presented to T. F. Tout ") to be due to a desire to lessen the risk of a City rising and to force the Londoners to plead in a strange place where they would feel less strong (*op. cit.* pp. 292–3).

[9] Higden (IX, p. 270) says the king's anger was increased because, failing to get the loan he wanted from London, he got it through a Lombard who

various matters ; one was the alleged contempt by the Londoners of the king's writ of summons to Nottingham;[1] according to the continuator of the *Eulogium Historiarum*,[2] the mayor, sheriffs and aldermen were accused of permitting the bakers, brewers and butchers of London to make excessive profits. It was planned, if they denied this charge, to prove it by a packed jury ; the continuator of Higden[3] declares that another reason for the king's anger was the fact that riots had recently taken place, caused by disputes between some of his officials and the Londoners. It is probable that these riots formed the main part of the charge of misgovernment of the City ; certainly this is the pretext that survived in London tradition[4] as the only cause of the king's action. It is unlikely, however, that the king would have taken so drastic an action for any reason less vital than the desire to obtain money of which he had been unable to get possession by other means. Certainly there is no mention, either in the City records or on the Patent Rolls, of any loan to the king on the part of the City itself or of any individual citizen between June 1388 and September 1397.[5] The fate of Brembre probably deterred individual merchants from entering into close relationship with the Government :[6] more important than this, the chief interest

had borrowed the sum from the very Londoners who had told the King they were too poor to lend it to him. Walsingham (*Hist. Ang.* II, pp. 207–8) adds that they later half-killed the Lombard for his action ; but he never believes anything good of the Londoners, accusing them, among other things, of pride, avarice, infidelity and support of Lollards.

[1] *Cal. L.B.H*, pp. 378–9 ; Higden, IX, p. 272.   [2] III, p. 367.

[3] Higden, IX, p. 268. For further details see below, pp. 106–7.

[4] Harl. 565 (ed. Nicholas), pp. 79, 80 ; The Brut (ed. Brie), pp. 345–8, cf. Gregory's *Chronicle* (ed. Gairdner), p. 94 ; Grafton (pp. 458–9) and Fabyan (edition of 1811), pp. 536–7.

[5] Mr. Steel, in his second article on English Government Finance 1377–1413, claims that Richard did not need to borrow in the nineties, and that this accounts for the fact that the citizens of London only lent him £21,363 12s. 7d. between 1389–99, as against £44,682 12s. 0½d. between 1377–89—but he owns that only £100 of the 10,000 marks lent in August 1397 was ever repaid (*E.H.R.* October 1936, p. 591).

[6] Is this perhaps one reason why Venour lends £4988 in Mr. Steel's first period, and only £906 in the second ? *Ibid.* p. 591. Venour, senior, died before the end of 1395. His son, also called William, seems to have dealt in tin as well as wool (*Cal. P. and M.R.* 1381–1412, pp. 234, 285-6-7 ; *Cal. P.R.* 1397, p. 158).

of the mercantile community, now as earlier, was the protection of commerce, particularly in the English Channel; with the conclusion of the truce with France,[1] however, it became apparent that there was no chance, at any rate while the truce lasted, of the Government making any effort in that direction ; there was, therefore, in their eyes, no reason for advancing money to the Crown. It is true that in August 1397, when the City advanced nearly £7000 to the king,[2] this truce was still in force ; but the incidents of the summer of 1392 are quite sufficient to account for this loan ; it is not likely that the City capitalists would wish to run the risk of another £10,000 fine, as well as the temporary loss of their liberties, by a second refusal, particularly as the demand was made of them at a time when the king was at the height of his power, and it seemed as if there were no man, and no party either, with courage enough to oppose him. Further, there is reason to believe that an attack was being made at this time on one of the privileges of the City—that of recording proceedings of the City Courts, when these were called into the King's Court by a writ of error, by word of mouth of the recorder, instead of in writing, and after an interval of at least forty days for consultation.[3] If this were so, it would be an additional reason for conciliating the king.[4]

To return to 1392, it would be of considerable interest to discover what part, if any, was played by the great land-owners in the humiliation of the Londoners in that year. Unfortunately it is almost impossible to get any evidence on the subject except from the chroniclers, and such evidence as there is, is not entirely unconflicting. According to the London tradition[5] the origin of the disturbance was as

---

[1] Proclaimed in the City July 1389 (*Cal. L.B.H*, p. 342) and renewed May 1392 (*ibid.* p. 377) just before the king's seizure of the liberties of the City.

[2] *Cal. P.R.* 1396–99, p. 180 ; cf. *Cal. L.B.H*, p. 438.

[3] The City was forced to assert this right at least three times, and perhaps four, in 1397, and possibly twice in 1398, see *Cal. P. and M.R.* 1381–1412, pp. 243–4, 245, 250, 250–1, 253, 255.

[4] In 1392, according to Walsingham, some of the privileges of London had been ratified, some permitted, some condemned (*Hist. Angl.* II, p. 210).

[5] See above, p. 105.

follows : a baker's man with a basket of " horse-bread " came to serve his master's customers in Fleet Street ; in Salisbury Alley a servant of the Bishop of Salisbury took a loaf from the basket and broke the man's head with a dagger when he tried to retrieve it ; the inhabitants of the street then made an effort to make the bishop's servant a prisoner, for breaking the peace, but his fellow-servants rescued him and took him into the bishop's house ; a crowd collected and attempted a forcible entry to secure the man.[1] Even after the mayor and sheriffs arrived the crowd increased, and the City officials found it difficult to disperse, failing to do so until the gates were already nearly broken in. The bishop himself was at Windsor at the time and the report made to him seems to have been considerably worse than the actual facts. John Waltham, then bishop, was also the Treasurer, and although, as Keeper of the Privy Seal, he had been one of those appointed to try those accused by the Lords Appellant in 1387-88,[2] was unconnected with any of the great families and is rather representative of the professional type of king's minister whose sympathy was seldom with the opposition to the Crown.[3] It is unlikely that he was popular with the merchant community of London, for in the first Parliament of Henry IV, petitions[4] were successfully presented by the Commons against the compulsory sealing of bales of cloth and excessive duty on wines, both of which had been imposed by his authority. He was not, however, a member of the Commission which tried the mayor, sheriffs and aldermen for misgovernment. This was representative of more than one party, as on it sat not only Gloucester and Nottingham but the Duke of York and Richard's half-brother, John Holland ; the last is declared by Higden[5] to have taken Waltham's part against the Londoners, together with the Duke of Lancaster : in another chronicle the Chancellor, Thomas Arundel, Archbishop of York, is said to have joined the Treasurer in complaint to the king.[6,7] Though it is

[1] Who is supposed to have been called Walter Romayne.
[2] *Rot. Parl.* III, p. 229.   [3] See his life in the *D.N.B.*
[4] *Rot. Parl.* III, pp. 437 and 448.
[5] Higden, IX, p. 268.   [6] Harl. 565, pp. 79–80.
[7] The article on Thomas Arundel in the *D.N.B.* suggests that he may have been behind the transfer of the Court of Common Pleas to the seat of his archiepiscopate in May (*Cal. Cl.R.* 1389–92, p. 565).

impossible to tell how far the appointments to the Commission were merely formal, with the real business of the Commission left to its legal members,[1] they at least indicate that these lords offered no opposition to the king on the question. Walsingham, however, declares that it was chiefly through the influence of the Duke of Gloucester[2] that Richard relented towards the Londoners (though their splendid gifts had weight with him), and that he was restrained from his original intention to destroy the inhabitants of the City altogether[3] by the persuasion of John of Gaunt— a statement which it is difficult to reconcile either with that of the continuator of Higden,[4] or with John of Gaunt's usual attitude towards the Londoners. That John of Gaunt had financial relations with the Londoners at this time is true, and they were of a somewhat unexpected and mysterious character, and are not paralleled at any other period of the duke's career for which the record of his financial dealings survives. In the accounts for 1392–93 of the Receiver-General of the Duchy of Lancaster,[5] there is a list of sums received in payment, or part payment, of money which the duke had advanced to the persons concerned the year before.[6] Some of these persons belong to John of Gaunt's own class, Henry Percy and Alianora, Duchess of Gloucester, being included among them, but twenty of them are London citizens, and the total amount paid over by these twenty, together with three non-Londoners, partners with one or other of them in this

---

[1] The two Chief Justices, Clopton and Thirnyng. Two other members of the Commission were Sir Richard Stury and Sir Lewis Clifford, both prominent as Lollards, according to Walsingham (*Hist. Angl.* II, pp. 159, 216), and the former one of the king's supporters in 1387 (*ibid.* p. 156).

[2] *Hist. Angl.* II, p. 209.

[3] " Meditatus est exercitum congregasse et in civitatem irruisse cum impetu et cives sub coelo delevisse " (*ibid.* p. 210). He describes the magnificent reception given later to the king by the City and the disgust of some of the nobles at his reconciliation with the Londoners and the fact that the fine was excused (*ibid.* pp. 210–11).

[4] See above, p. 107.

[5] Duchy of Lancaster Records, Accounts Various, Bundle III, Number 2.

[6] All the items are bracketed together, with the following note—Recept' denar' alias per dominum prestitor' in anno preced' et hoc anno resolut'. The accounts run from February to February.

matter, is more than £1500. Of this, Sir John Cobham and three Londoners[1] paid £134 6s. 8d. in part payment of a debt of £250, four[2] other citizens £66 13s. 4d. in part payment of twice that sum " lent them by the lord (duke) to the use of the Abbess of Barking," and William Venour and William his son £500 in part payment of £1000.[3] Venour was, of course, one of the aldermen at the time of the confiscation of the City's franchise, and he was also deputy of Sir Edward Dalyngrigge in July 1392.[4] Another of the aldermen, William Brampton, and Thomas Newenton, one of the men whom Richard appointed sheriffs in place of those whom he had deposed, are recorded as having paid back £300 to the duke in this year. In the Receiver-General's Accounts for 1393–94,[5] there is the following entry,[6] referring to the other sheriff appointed by the king : " Item paiez a Gilbert Maighfeld and Thomas Grast citezines de Londres par voie dapprest par lettre du garrant, etc. £200." It is tempting to connect at least some of these transactions with the political events of the time, but in the absence of other evidence it is impossible to explain any such connection. It is not even clear whether these are to be regarded as ordinary loans, or whether the citizens in question may not have been acting as the duke's bankers, in some sense or other.

It is not necessary, however, to find evidence for the

---

[1] Hugh Sprot, Richard Willisdon and John Norwich ; the sum is paid by the hands of William Venour.

[2] William Scharpyng, vintner, William Louth, John Moustre and John Maydeston.

[3] John Sewale Stok-fishmonger and John Esmond paid back £200 in full, John Hankon (?) and John Letherede £10, Robert de Parys and Richard Merlowe £200, Robert Basshey, Thomas Davy (?) and Thomas Exton £66 13s. 4d. and Thomas Duke and Giles Yonge £26 13s. 4d. lent them for the use of Agnes, once wife of Richard Haryng, knight. Yonge was from Berkshire and Hankon from Yarmouth. All the others were Londoners. £200 was also paid back by Bartholomew Bosan, merchant of Lucca.

[4] Cal. P. and M.R. 1381–1412, pp. 182–3.

[5] Records of the Duchy of Lancaster, Accounts Various, Bundle 32, Membrane 21. This bundle is classed in Lists and Indexes No. 14 as (? 2–3 Ric. II) but the manuscript itself is clearly dated 17–18 Ric. II. (The reference has lately been corrected in the P.R.O. Literary Search Room copy of Lists and Indexes No. 14.)

[6] In the second section, running from February 2 to August 10.

existence of any kind of an alliance between John of Gaunt
and the Londoners in order to account for the support that
they gave to his son when he claimed the throne in 1399.
It is clear that they were then animated, not so much by
any gratitude, or by hopes inspired by Henry, as by hatred
of Richard. The strength of this feeling is emphasised by
nearly all the contemporary chroniclers. The writer of the
Chronique de la Traïson declares that while Richard was
Henry's captive at Coventry, a deputation arrived from
London to beg for the execution of Richard before he is
brought any further,[1] while the same writer lays stress
on the welcome extended by the Londoners to Henry when
he approached their City[2] and on the share they took in
demanding him as king in Parliament.[3] Adam of Usk[4]
gives an account of a visit of three of the aldermen and fifty
of the citizens of London to Henry at Chester ; they
declared on their arrival that the City had searched for
Richard at Westminster and, not finding him, had ordered
three of his special counsellors into custody till the Parliament met. An almost identical story is told by that London
chronicler who has given us such a full and accurate account
of the Parliament of 1399 ;[5] while Otterbourne records a
request of Richard's that the citizens of London should not
be allowed to see him while a prisoner at Westminster,
because he was convinced they would exult so greatly over
his downfall.[6] Some of the reasons for this detestation in
which Richard was held have already been described. Of
twenty-four members of the Court of Aldermen of 1399,
seventeen[7] had been present at Nottingham in 1392 when
the king seized the liberties of the City into his hand.
That these proceedings had aroused fear as well as hatred
is clear from the petition of the Londoners on the subject

---

[1] *Chronique de la Traïson* (ed. Williams), p. 61.

[2] *Ibid.* p. 62.   [3] *Ibid.* p. 68.

[4] *Chronicon Adae de Usk* (ed. E. Maunde Thompson), p. 28. Usk was an
eye-witness of these events (Introd. p. vii).

[5] The writer of 1 Julius B.II, printed by Kingsford in his *Chronicle of
London*, p. 19.

[6] *Chronicle of Thomas Otterbourne* (ed. Hearne), p. 209.

[7] Nine as aldermen, eight as Commoners of the " more sufficient " class
(*Cal. L.B.H*, pp. 377-8).

in the first Parliament of Henry IV,[1] claiming that
individual officers of the City should suffer for their own
actions, and not the City as a whole, grounding their
request on various earlier charters.[2] Richard's actions during
the last three years of his reign only intensified the senti-
ments of the Londoners. According to the writer of the
Chronique de la Traïson, Henry of Lancaster on landing
sent a letter to them declaring it to be Richard's intention
to make himself more absolute than English king had ever
been, by foreign assistance, and to use his power to get
limitless sums of money out of the prominent citizens,
aldermen and merchants of the towns of England.[3] This
letter may not be authentic[4] but there can be no doubt
that the argument employed in it was that which was
most calculated to weigh with the citizens, for they, with
many other cities and towns had been forced to sign " blank
charters " rendering them liable to furnish Richard with
whatever sums of money he should demand from them.[5]
To this the Rolls of Parliament testify.[6] There is no mention
of such a transaction in Letter Book H, but it is possible
that it may have been recorded on one of the folios which
are missing.[7] The " remembrances appellez Raggemans ou

---

[1] *Rot. Parl.* III, pp. 442–3.

[2] The result was a statute which, after reciting that of 1354 goes on to
say that " our Lord the King, considering the good and lawful behaviour
of the mayor, sheriffs and aldermen, and of all the Commonalty of the same
City of London towards him " has ordained that the penalty in the case for
which the Statute provides shall be decided by the justices in each separate
case, and shall not necessarily consist of the two fines and the confiscation of
the franchise (*Statutes of the Realm*, II, pp. 117–8). It had already been enacted
(in 1393–94) that the Statute of 1354 was not to be held to apply to erroneous
judgments in the City Courts, for which there was already a means of appeal
to the Justices in Error sitting at St. Martin-le-Grand (*Statutes of the Realm*,
II, p. 91). (The City was not again " Taken into the King's hand " for
nearly 300 years—in the reign of Charles II.) Henry IV also, in 1400, issued
a writ to sheriffs, mayors, bailiffs, etc., throughout the kingdom not to
molest citizens of London in their chartered rights (*Cal. L.B.I*, p. 13).

[3] *Chronique de la Traïson*, p. 35.

[4] There is no trace of it in the City Records.

[5] Mr. Mead speaks of £1000 having been paid over by London because of
the " blank charters " ; see also Harl. 565, p. 83, and Gregory's *Chronicle*,
pp. 98–101.   [6] *Rot. Parl.* III, p. 432.

[7] See *Cal. L.B.H*, Introd. pp. lvi–lvii and 450—some of the folios are
blank, some mutilated, some missing.

blanches Chartres nadgairs enseallez en la Citee de Loundres"
were returned to those who had signed them [1] after the
first Parliament of Henry IV,[2] and if a record or records
of these " charters " had been entered in the Letter Book,
it is quite probable that they would have been destroyed
at the same time as the originals. This grievance weighed
not only on the merchant capitalists but also on the small
masters, through the exactions imposed on their misteries.[3]

According to the writer of Harleian 565 Richard imposed
his will on London at this time by armed men from Cheshire,
in spite of the efforts made by the Archbishop of Canterbury
and the Bishop of London on their behalf—the result being
" a grete fray in Fryday Strete on a Night in there innes."[4]

To these injuries was added another, resented bitterly
by all classes. This was the restoration, made by Richard
just before he set out for Ireland,[5] of all the privileges of
the free fishmongers, not only their monopoly of retail
trade, but the immunities enjoyed by their " halimot." [6]
It seems incredible that the king could have imagined that
the fishmongers were possessed of such power that it could
be to his advantage to conciliate them with the certain
result of offending the rest of London ; that state of
affairs had almost, if not quite, passed away by the time of
his accession. He could not have done a more unpopular
thing. By restoring the privileges of the " halimot " he
angered the governing class and roused craft jealousy,

---

[1] *Rot. Parl.* iii, p. 432.

[2] See *Eulog. Hist.* p. 387, for the City's pained surprise that Henry should
ask for a loan after all his promises. He proved a far worse debtor than Richard
had been. See Mr. Steel's second article on Government finance, *E.H.R.*
October 1936, pp. 590–3.

[3] See H. G. Rosedale, *The Worshipful Company of Horners*, p. 19. " And
thanne after the presentacion of the said supplication ther were made mony
blank charteres and all the men of every crafte of the said Cite as well as all
manere servaunts and maisters were charged to come to the Guylde halle to
sette her seales to the said blank charteres " (said to be from a newly discovered
document under date 1397). The statement on p. 20 that the king took the
City into his hands in 1397 is quite unfounded.

[4] Harl. 565, p. 83.

[5] *Cal. L.B.H*, pp. 447–8—on 9 May 1399 ; Richard sailed on the 29th
of that month.

[6] As has been stated above, the Letters Patent containing this grant were
revoked in the Parliament of 1399.

while a rise in the price of fish is sufficient to account for
any hostility shown the fallen king on the part of the mass
of the population of the City.[1] It is this affair of the fishmongers alone which connects the welcome given by the
Londoners to Henry of Lancaster with his father's protégé,
John of Northampton,[2] for in all other respects it is a London
which has acquiesced in the entire defeat of Northampton's
aims which welcomes Henry with such enthusiasm.

[1] Fabyan declares that the mob intended to seize Richard outside London
and murder him, but were prevented by the City officials (p. 546).

[2] Northampton had been dead over two years. His will was proved on
5 January 1397 (*Commiss. of London Registers, Courtney*, 406–7).

CHAPTER VIII

GENERAL CONCLUSIONS

THE first and last impression that a detailed study of London under Richard II gives is of an exceeding complexity of interests, personal and corporate, giving rise to one conflict after another, in which motives of groups, and still more of individuals, are very difficult to distinguish. At first sight there seem to be two distinct groups, but each of these was an alliance of smaller groups, with different and, at times, conflicting aims, rather than a homogeneous whole. That party of which John of Northampton was the head had for its object the destruction of the virtual monopoly of political power within the City held by the merchant capitalists. The backbone of the party was certainly the small master class, the class from which the majority of the common councillors was drawn, but which never, in ordinary circumstances, gained representation in the Court of Aldermen, far less in the office of mayor or sheriff. This monopoly they first attempted to break by securing compulsory annual election of aldermen and the nomination by the misteries of common councillors who alone might elect the mayor and one sheriff ; secondly, they disabled all victuallers from holding judicial office ;[1] finally, when their leader had been defeated in the mayoralty election in 1383 they attempted to gain their ends by disturbance and riot. With the arrest of that leader and two of his three most prominent subordinates,[2] however, the party appears to have lost nearly all its courage, and though it kept up the conflict for a few years longer it did so only intermittently, and finally acquiesced not only in the reversal of all the constitutional measures it had established, but also in the

[1] This would, of course, include the office of alderman as well as those of mayor and sheriff.

[2] The third, William Essex, disappeared from the City for good some time between February 1383–84 and the September of that year (*Cal. L.B.H*, p. 304).

establishment of even greater control by the aldermen over the composition of their own body, by the ordinances which forced the wards first to present two, and later four names, out of which the mayor and aldermen should choose their new colleague. That this party of Northampton's was drawn almost entirely from the non-victualling, and very largely from the smaller, misteries was due to two things. First, the most prominent if not the majority, of the merchant capitalists in London at this time belonged either to the grocers' or the fishmongers' mistery as they had in the generation just past to the vintners' or fishmongers', and as they did in the early part of the next century to the grocers' or mercers'. The three most outstanding names of those three periods are John Stodeye, vintner, John Philpot, grocer, and Richard Whittington, mercer. The reason for this is not far to seek, for the very nature of the commodities in which they dealt made the successful members of these misteries merchants, as opposed to the craftsmen of the smaller misteries. This is not to say that there were not capitalists too in the greater non-victualling misteries—the drapers, the skinners and the goldsmiths as well as the mercers. These ranged themselves beside their fellow capitalists of the victualling misteries in opposition to their fellow-members who were solely craftsmen, and supported their policy of subordinating the misteries to the governing body of the City.[1] The bitterness of this opposition of interest was lessened by the custom of the rich citizens of buying land outside the City and of becoming absorbed in the lesser aristocracy by at least the third generation ; this destroyed any tendency, if such existed, of the establishment of anything like a hereditary oligarchy, such as existed in some Continental cities, and prevented widespread discontent by permitting the continuous rise of new men to power.[2] Nor, although

[1] That this control of the misteries was a deliberate policy on the part of the capitalists is shown by the complaints of the crafts, in the petitions alluded to above, that Brembre had taken away their charters and refused to restore them—but his policy was not opposed at the time or afterwards, so far as we have record, by his non-victualling colleagues on the Court of Aldermen.

[2] These, however, often came from outside the City, or belonged to the second generation of such Londoners.

there are conflicts between misteries, one of whom was practically dependent for its market on another, because of the relation of their craft processes to one another, is there any sign of such cleavage between Brembre's party of merchants and Northampton's of craftsmen ; the tension was therefore not so great as in some Continental cities, where the party in power was composed of manufacturers and bankers, the employers of the classes who opposed them in city politics. Though the merchants of the London non-victualling misteries allied themselves with those of the victualling misteries, the small men of these misteries did not ally themselves with the small masters of the non-victualling misteries, as they might have been logically expected to do. This is accounted for by the measures to secure cheap food taken by Northampton and his party, not only for their own benefit, but to rouse the enthusiasm of the lowest orders of Londoners, the journeymen and the inferior classes of workmen who were not even organised into misteries. When it came to a question of their own privileges as masters against the aims of the journeymen, however, they were not willing to concede anything at all. This is shown particularly with regard to the efforts of the journeymen to establish fraternities of their own. The chief effort of Northampton's party in the campaign for cheap food was that directed against the free fishmongers, and it was on this question, and on the question of free trade in victuals generally, that the party opposed to Northampton was chiefly divided. The retail victualler was naturally whole-heartedly opposed to any permission at all being granted to the " foreigner " or non-freeman, to retail his own particular commodity in the City. This side of the question hardly affected the capitalist victuallers, with the partial exception of the fishmongers, at all, and they,[1] when in office, dealt out as strict justice to the fraudulent or profiteering retailer of food as their opponents. As a result, the small men among the victuallers were far more the enemies of Northampton than the supporters of the capitalists ; the inquisitions taken after the Risings of 1381 show them to have been a turbulent class, one of

---

[1] Including the fishmongers, e.g. Walworth.

the chief reasons for their disorderly character probably being the continual suspicion in which they were held by their fellow-citizens.[1] Within the class of merchant capitalists itself, however, there was division on the question of the free fishmongers. With their monopoly of the retail trade the fishmongers' fellow-merchants were probably not disposed to interfere, though events showed that they were not prepared to maintain it against the hostility of the majority of the citizens. On the other hand, they were most anxious to destroy the privilege which the fishmongers possessed of having all disputes which concerned their mistery settled in their own court instead of in those of the City. To effect this destruction the older aldermen were willing to co-operate even with John of Northampton.

All these issues were complicated by personal rivalries among the capitalists,[2] arising out of a desire for the office of mayor, and by craft jealousies, particularly between the goldsmiths and other misteries.[3]

As to the relations between the Londoners and the Church, while the rich citizens lavished their wealth—particularly at their death—on individual churches and religious foundations, when a question of privilege or of the jurisdiction of the Church Courts arose, their attitude was almost as hostile as that of their successors, the merchants of the sixteenth century. The Londoners had achieved so much already by the fourteenth century that there is no real struggle with the clergy in this period. One reason for their early success was very probably because their bishop was frequently a royal official who thought less of the claims of his See than of the finances of the central government.

[1] General conditions, over which they had practically no control, made it exceedingly difficult for them to keep their goods in a sound condition without destroying their appetising qualities, but their customers seem to have made no allowances for these difficulties.

[2] And very probably among the lesser men in less important connections, but the records here do not give enough detail to make a clear picture.

[3] The "rancour" which existed between the goldsmiths and the grocers may have been partly due to the fact that the latter occasionally held the office of "changeour" to the king—but this is only a partial explanation, as the rank and file of the goldsmiths cannot have been affected by it.

In its contact with this central government the influence of London at this time showed itself to be rather negative than positive in its effects. To this result the divisions within the City largely contributed, for at three crises of the period—at the time of the " Good " Parliament, during the Risings of 1381,[1] and above all when the Lords Appellant were triumphant—the rulers of the City temporised and finally threw in their lot with the party which appeared to be the stronger, principally because they feared outside support might be given to their enemies within the City.

A second factor, however, was of great importance. It is clear that the capitalists realised to the full the necessity of supplying the Government with money if the war with France—which to them meant mainly an attack on piracy —was to be carried on successfully. It is equally clear, how-ever, that they did not at all realise the need of the Govern-ment for steady financial support in time of peace if it was to be a government in anything more than name. The great landowners appeared to them at the beginning of Richard's reign as men who mismanaged the military and naval operations against France which they were financing, and as customers whose displeasure was not to be despised. Later they regarded them as a menace to the independence and security of the City, on account of their forces of armed men, and, as such, to be conciliated as far as possible. As a menace—and more than a menace—to any sort of centralised government, they never seem to have regarded them. Even if they had, the time had not yet come when they would regard centralised government as something worth paying for and fighting for. On the other side, though the Government of Richard's minority seems to have realised the importance of conciliating the Londoners, Richard himself did not do so, as his conduct in 1392 and again in 1399 testifies. He had, however, as some justifica-tion for his point of view, a memory of their failure to support him against the Lords Appellant, when he had for some time acted so as to please them in every possible way.

[1] To a lesser extent then, however.

As for the great landowners, they resented exceedingly any interference of the merchants in matters of government, though they were willing enough to secure their financial support when they happened to be directing the affairs of the country. In City politics as such they were profoundly uninterested, though they were capable of turning City factions to their own profit, and sometimes took a personal interest—based in some cases, perhaps, on financial considerations [1]—in some of the leaders of these factions.

The knights of the shire, again, were indifferent to City affairs as such, but it was easy to convince them that the poverty of the Government and the increased taxation were due to the evil practices of the merchants who financed the Crown ; co-operation between the knights and the Londoners, therefore, is of rare occurrence.

London, however, by the end of the fourteenth century, had reached a stage of development, that of the firm establishment of government by a mercantile oligarchy,[2] which made it able to strike effectively in general politics, unhampered by serious disturbance within itself ; it would do so as soon as it rose above the absorption in local interests and ignorance of the real position of the Crown which had made it in that century akin to the rest of England. It had to realise that it had any concern with general politics before it could use the great power it now possessed.

[1] This certainly does not seem to apply to John of Gaunt's relations with his namesake of Northampton, however.

[2] This had come about by the very struggle itself of the men of moderate means against the governing class.

APPENDIX I

Family connections of John Stodeye, vintner, died 1376—based on the Hustings Rolls, Plea and Memoranda Rolls, Documents concerning Vintners' Hall and Stow's Survey—(the last only for Philpot's first wife). The order of age of Stodeye's daughters is conjectural.

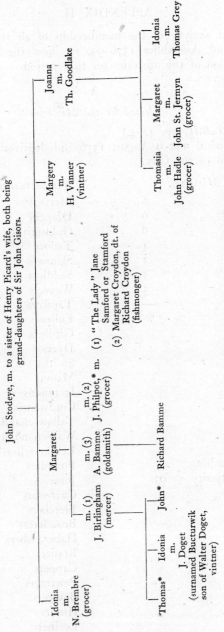

John Stodeye, m. to a sister of Henry Picard's wife, both being grand-daughters of Sir John Gisors.

* Thomas and John died before their mother. John Philpot had a son, John Philpot, mercer (*H.R.*, 135:24).

121

APPENDIX II.

Detailed analysis of the membership of all recorded Common Councils and Assemblies 1376–99, to show the variation in the representation of the misteries for that period.

A

Elected by the Misteries

(1) (*Cal. L.B.H*, pp. 42–4.)

This council met 9 August 1376 and deprived John Pecche of the freedom of the City.

Victualling Misteries.		*Non-victualling Misteries.*	
Grocers	6	Mercers	6
Fishmongers	6	Drapers	6
Vintners	6	Goldsmiths	6
Brewers	4	Tailors	6
Bakers	2	Skinners	6
Salters	3	Saddlers	4
Butchers	3	Weavers	4
	—	Tapicers	4
	30	Fullers	4
		Girdlers	4
		Dyers	4
		Smiths	4
		Masons	4
		Ironmongers	4
		Cordwainers	4
		Tallow-chandlers	3
		Wax-chandlers	2
		Leathersellers	2
Non-victualling		Founders	2
majority = 93.		Joiners	2
		Curreours	2
		Fletchers	2
		Brouderers	2
		Haberdashers	2
		Brasiers	2
		Cappers	2
		Pewterers	2
		Bowyers	2
		Hurers	2
		Loriners	2
		Horners	2

Non-victualling Misteries.

Armourers	2
Cutlers	2
Spurriers	2
Plomers	2
Shearmen	2
Painters	2
Pouchmakers	2
Woodmongers	2
Pinners	2
Tanners	2
	——
	123

(2) (*Cal. L.B.H*, p. 59.)

This council met 6 March 1376–77 and ordained that no alderman who had ever been removed from office for ' reasonable cause ' should ever be re-elected.

Victualling Misteries.

Grocers	6
Fishmongers	6
Vintners	6
	——
	18

Non-victualling
    majority = 28.

Non-victualling Misteries.

Mercers	6
Drapers	6
Skinners	6
Tailors	6
Saddlers	4
Haberdashers	4
Armourers	2
Girdlers	4
Cordwainers	4
Chandlers	4
	——
	46

(3) (*Cal. P. and M.R.* 1381–1412, pp. 29–30.)

This council met during the first mayoralty of John de Northampton, 1381–82.

Victualling Misteries.

Grocers	6
Vintners	6
Fishmongers	6
Butchers	6
Brewers	4
Salters	2
Bakers	2
	——
	32

Non-victualling Misteries.

Drapers	6
Mercers	6
Goldsmiths	6
Tailors	6
Skinners	4
Saddlers	4
Cordwainers	4
Haberdashers	4
Smiths	4

Non-victualling Misteries.

Armourers	2
Ironmongers	2
Shearmen	2
Weavers	3
Dyers	2
Cutlers	2
Girdlers	2
Curriers	2
Fullers	2
Founders	2
Brouderers	2
Fustours	2
Pewterers	2
Woodmongers	2
Plomers	2
Tapicers	2
Leathersellers	2
Painters	2
Tanners (illegible)	
Hurers	2
Joiners	2
White Tawyers	2
Loriners	2
Bowyers	2
Fletchers	2
Hatters (illegible)	
Horners	2
Spurriers	2
Pouchmakers	2
Pinners	2
Masons	1
Tallow-chandlers	4
Wax-chandlers	2

Non-victualling
majority = 76 at least
probably 78.

———
108

B

Elected by the Wards

(1) (*Cal. P. and M.R.* 1381–1412, pp. 53–4.)

This council met 11 June 1384 and all the members severally bore witness that John de Northampton was responsible for all the rioting and conspiracies in the City which had occurred since he ceased to be mayor.

Victualling Misteries.

Vintners	7
Fishmongers	4
Grocers	3
Butchers	2
Hostillers	1
Pulters	1
	—
	18

Non-victualling
  majority = 23.

There are no representatives from Bassishaw, and it has been found impossible to identify the mistery of one man, John Raynard.

Non-victualling Misteries.

Skinners	6
Drapers	6
Woolmen	5
Tailors	4
Goldsmiths	3
Weavers	2
Ironmongers	2
Tapicers	2
Saddlers	2
Corders	1
Haberdashers	1
Cutlers	1
Painters	1
Fynours	1
Smiths	1
Armourers	1
Woodmongers	1
Bellmakers	1
	—
	41

(2) (*Cal. L.B.H*, pp. 237–44.)

This council met 31 August 1384 and unanimously agreed to pray the king to punish Northampton, no one saying a word to the contrary though invited to do so fearlessly.

Victualling Misteries.

Grocers	21
Fishmongers	17
Vintners	16
Brewers	6
Butchers	5
Hostillers	4
Salters	4
Pie Bakers	2
Bakers	1
Pulters	11
Maltmongers	1
Brewers	1
Bladers	1
(Corn Merchants)	
	—
	80

Non-victualling Misteries.

Skinners	19
Drapers	17
Mercers	17
Goldsmiths	12
Tailors	12
Ironmongers	7
Woolmen	7
Saddlers	5
Cordwainers	4
Haberdashers	3
Cutlers	3
Woodmongers	3
Curreours	3
Girdlers	3
Tapicers	2
Painters	2

Non-victualling Misteries.

Smiths	2
Weavers	2
Armourers	2
Dyers	2
Masons	2
Corders	1
Fynours	1
Bellmakers	1
Founders	1
Furnagers	1
Peuterers	1
Coopers	1
Sheathers	1
Joiners	1
Shearmen	1
Brouderers	1
Corsours	1
Plomers	1
Jewellers	1
Potters	1
Chandlers	9
	—
	153

It has been found impossible to trace the misteries of 21 councillors. The non-victualling majority, therefore, lies between 52 and 94.

(3) (*Cal. P. and M.R* 1381–1412, pp. 84–9.)
This council met 13 October 1384 and with 231 other citizens elected Brembre mayor for the ensuing year.

Victualling Misteries.

Grocers	9
Vintners	8
Fishmongers	8
Butchers	3
Brewers	1
Pulters	1
Hostillers	1
	—
	31

Non-victualling Misteries.

Drapers	8
Skinners	8
Mercers	8
Woolmen	5
Ironmongers	5
Goldsmiths	4
Tailors	3
Tapicers	2
Saddlers	2
Coppersmiths	1
Woodmongers	2
Cutlers	1
Brouderers	1
Painters	1
Fynours	1

	Non-victualling Misteries.	
	Corders	I
	Armourers	I
Non-victualling	Founders	I
majority = 31.	Bellmakers	I
	Furnagers	I
	Chandlers	3
	Weavers	2
		—
		62

(4) (*Cal. P. and M.R.* 1381–1412, pp. 54–5.)

This council met 25 March 1384–85 and petitioned the king for Northampton's execution.

Victualling Misteries.		Non-victualling Misteries.	
Vintners	8	Skinners	7
Grocers	4	Mercers	6
Fishmongers	4	Tailors	5
Pulters	I	Drapers	5
Butchers	I	Goldsmiths	4
	—	Woolmen	4
	18	Ironmongers	3
		Tapicers	2
		Woodmongers	2
		Corders	I
		Haberdashers	I
		Saddlers	I
		Painters	I
		Fynours	I
Non-victualling		Weavers	I
majority = 34.		Armourers	I
		Fullers	I
		Chaloners	I
(There are no councillors		Brouderers	I
from Bassishaw.)		Furnagers	I
		Founders	I
		Chandlers	2
			—
			52

(5) (*Cal. P. and M.R.* 1381–1412, pp. 91–2.)

A council held 8 Richard II.

Victualling Misteries.		Non-victualling Misteries.	
Vintners	8	Drapers	10
Fishmongers	8	Skinners	7

Victualling Misteries.		*Non-victualling Misteries.*	
Grocers	10	Mercers	7
Butchers	2	Woolmen	5
Pulters	1	Goldsmiths	5
Hostillers	1	Tailors	4
	—	Ironmongers	3
	30	Saddlers	2
		Tapicers	2
		Weavers	2
		Woodmongers	2
		Bellmakers	1
		Founders	1
		Furnagers	1
		Corders	1
Non-victualling		Fynours	1
majority = 33.		Painters	1
		Armourers	1
		Brouderers	1
		Chaloners	1
		Cutlers	1
		Cordwainers	1
		Chandlers	3
			—
			63

(6) (*Cal. P. and M.R.* 1381–1412, pp. 122–4.)
Council held 1386.

Victualling Misteries.		*Non-victualling Misteries.*	
Grocers	9	Drapers	8
Vintners	8	Mercers	7
Fishmongers	7	Woolmen	7
Butchers	3	Skinners	6
Taverners	1	Tailors	5
Hostillers	1	Goldsmiths	5
Pulters	1	Ironmongers	4
	—	Woodmongers	3
	30	Tapicers	2
Non-victualling		Weavers	2
majority = 34.		Armourers	1
		Cutlers	1
		Chaloners	1
		Fynours	1
		Painters	1
		Broderers	1

Non-victualling Misteries.

Hatters	1
Corders	1
Cordwainers	1
Furnagers	1
Bellmakers	1
Founders	1
Jewellers	1
Saddlers	1
Chandlers	2
	—
	65

(7) (*Cal. L.B.H*, pp. 279–81).

Assembly of March 1385–86 which declared on oath it would be against the peace of the City for Northampton, More and Norbury to approach the City as near as forty miles. It is possible that these men were not elected by the wards, but simply chosen by the mayor, and they are called "The best of the folk of the City and suburbs to attend in the Chamber of Common Council."

Victualling Misteries.

Grocers	19
Fishmongers	14
Vintners	9
Brewers	5
Butchers	3
Pulters	3
Piebakers	2
Bakers	2
Hostillers	2
Salters	2
Bladers	1
Fruiters	1
	—
	63

There are 10 whose misteries cannot be traced, so that non-victualling majority lies between—27 and 47.

Non-victualling Misteries.

Drapers	10
Skinners	10
Mercers	10
Goldsmiths	9
Woolmen	7
Woodmongers	4
Tailors	4
Ironmongers	4
Weavers	3
Cordwainers	3
Armourers	3
Saddlers	2
Brasiers	2
Carters	1
Glovers	1
Shearmen	1
Shethers	1
Girdlers	1
Founders	1
Bellmakers	1
Dyers	1
Brouderers	1
Painters	1
Masons	1

Non-victualling Misteries.

Furnagers	1
Cutlers	1
Corders	1
Jewellers	1
Fletchers	1
Paternostrers	1
Haberdashers	1
Pewterers	1
Chaloners	1
Coopers	1
Chandlers	8
	—
	100

(8) (*Cal. P. and M.R.* 1381–1412, pp. 132–3.)

Common Council of the mayoral year 1386–87. It was in April of this year that the mayor, aldermen and Common Council agreed that Northampton, More, Norbury and Essex should be for ever deprived of the freedom of the City (*Cal. L.B.H*, pp. 303–4).

Victualling Misteries.

Vintners	10
Grocers	8
Fishmongers	8
Butchers	3
Hostillers	2
(one excused)	
Salters	1
Pulters	1
	—
	33

Non-victualling
majority = 30.

Non-victualling Misteries.

Woolmen	9
Drapers	8
Skinners	6
Mercers	6
Goldsmiths	5
Tailors	5
Ironmongers	4
Woodmongers	3
Weavers	2
Tapicers	2
Fynours	1
Painters	1
Brouderers	1
Corders	1
Jewellers	1
Cordwainers	1
Saddlers	1
Bellmakers	1
Founders	1
Pewterers	1
Smiths	1
Chandlers	2
	—
	63

(9) (*Cal. L.B.H*, pp. 331–4.)

Council of 31 August 1388, which elected William Tonge and John Clenhand to sit in the Parliament of October 1388.

Victualling Misteries.		*Non-victualling Misteries.*	
Grocers	16	Drapers	20
Fishmongers	11	Skinners	16
Brewers	8	Mercers	9
Vintners	7	Goldsmiths	9
Butchers	4	Woolmen	7
Pulters	3	Ironmongers	7
Salters	2	Tailors	5
Hostillers	2	Weavers	3
Pie-Bakers	2	Cordwainers	3
Bakers	1	Cutlers	3
Fruiters	1	Woodmongers	2
Bladers	1	Shearmen	2
	—	Masons	2
	58	Painters	2
		Tanners	2
		Girdlers	2
		Tapicers	2
		Dyers	2
		Pewterers	2
The misteries of 27 of the council-		Haberdashers	1
lors cannot be discovered, so that		Paternosturs	1
the non-victualling majority is from		Armourers	1
38 to 92.		Joiners	1
		Smiths	1
		Hurers	1
		Brouderers	1
		Fullers	1
		Bellmakers	1
		Founders	1
		Barbers	1
		Furnagers	1
		Saddlers	1
		Brasiers	1
		Glovers	1
		Pouchmakers	1
		Chandlers	7
			—
			123

APPENDIX III

THE LONDON REBELS OF 1381

Table to show some differences between the list in the Rolls of Parliament and those in the City Records.

Class.	Rot. Parl.	City Records.
Wine Drawers	3	2
Taverners	1	0
Butchers	1	1
Butlers	1	0
Brewers	4	1
Corn Meters	1	1
Corn Peckers	1	1
Water Bearers	1	0
Servants	7	23
Apprentices	0	2
Joiners	0	1
Masons	0	1
Pouchmakers	0	2
Pinners	0	1
Cardmakers	0	1
Wiredrawers	0	1
Esquires	0	1
Carters	0	2
Woodmongers	0	1
Marberers	0	1
Grey Tawyers	0	1
Thresshers	0	1
Buckler Makers	0	1
Leather Dyers	0	1
Cooks	0	1
Women	0	3
Fourbours	0	1
Smiths	0	4
Weavers	11	4
Cobblers	4	2
Child Shoe-makers	1	0
Cordwainers	2	1
Fullers	4	5
Tailors	4	4

Class.	Rot. Parl.	City Records.
Saddlers	3	2
Cappers	3	2
Carpenters	4	1
Skinners	2	2
Goldsmiths	1	1
Spurriers	1	0
Tilers	2	1
Hosiers	1	0
Grinders	1	0
Shethers	1	0
Shearmen	2	0
" Waterledere "	1	0
Daubers	3	1
Dyers	3	2
Sawyers	2	0
Glovers	1	0
" Male makers "	1	0
Tinkers	1	0
Barbers	1	0
" Flexman "	1	0
Mattress Makers	1	1
Labourers	1	0
Clerks	1	0
" Travelying-man "	1	1
Boatmen	2	5
Porters	3	2
Undescribed	48	139
Not from London but from outlying districts.	13	5

APPENDIX IV

Transcript of part of Coram Rege Roll 507—being one of the inquisitions taken at the trial of John de Northampton. (See *Peasants' Rising and the Lollards*, p. 36.) This is the second inquisition, which Powell and Trevelyan do not print.

Item jurati dicunt quod die iovis undecimo die Febr' predicto quo die dictus Iohannes Norhampton fuit sub aresto in mansione predicti maioris ut predicitur idem Iohannes Bere in Bredstret in presencia multorum hominum ibidem existencium et audiencium dixit ad commovendum populum felonie contra dictum maiorem ex parte dicti Iohannis Norhampton talia verba. Est pudor et magnum scandalum pro omnibus in civitate Londonie quod Iohannes Norhampton noster superior et maior est taliter sub aresto in prisona detentus. Et dixit quod bonum esset ad querendum et deliberandum eum a dicta prisona. Et ad hoc faciendum promptus fuit et libenter adiuvaret dicto Iohanne Bere tunc sciente eundem Iohannem Norhampton tunc esse maiorem. Set quod dictus Nicholaus Brembre tunc extitit maior. Item per quandam aliam inquisicionem similiter present' extitit quod triduum proximum ante diem eleccionis dicti maioris videlicet ante diem translacionis Sancti Edwardi Regis anno septimo supradicto Iohannes Norhampton civis et pannarius dicte civitatis londonie et complices sui videlicet Willelmus Essex draper et Thomas Usk scryveyn principales attraxerunt sibi consencientes auxilientes consiliarios et fautores Iohannem More mercer Ricardum Norbury mercer Iohannem Wylardby taillor Willelmum Norton sadeler Iohannem Muntham joynour Iohannem Cole sadeler Iohannem Wilby taillour Iohannem Bliton squyer Iohannem Carbonell aurifabrum Iohannem Cheddar mercer Willelmum Bury mercer Iohannem Willesdon mercer Iohannem Gy mercer Robertum Pipot bowyer Iohannem Hydyngham hattere Iohannem Lincolle aurifabrum Thomam Depham sadeler Willelmum Tyngewyk aurifabrum Iohannem Vyne mercer Ricardum Brendewode draper Iohannem Constantyn cordewaner Thomam Everard mercer Thomam Kyngesbrigge cordewaner Stephanum Thorp aurifabrum Iohannem Dancastre copersmyth Iohannem Remes cordewaner Robertum Ryseby draper Iohannem Longe juniorem cordewaner Robertum Cumberton Thomam Lincolle draper Robertum Lincolle mercer Robertum Yorke cordewaner Iohannem Feraunt mercer Willelmum Bonere aurifabrum Robertum Seckford seriaunt Willelmum Waldiarn sadeler Willelmum Belhomme lethermonger et Willelmum Temple bladsmyth. Et cum ipsis conspiraverunt apud ecclesiam Sancti Thome de Acon london et apud aulam scissorum prope ecclesiam Sancti Antonii london et in aliis pluribus locis dicte civitatis et procuraverunt et incitaverunt populum tam de suis misteris quam de aliis in dicta civitate et se confederaverunt ad reeligendum ipsum Iohannem Norhampton maiorem dicte civitatis pro anno proximo tunc sequenti ubi tales conspiraciones procuraciones incitaciones et confederaciones percogitate sunt illicite contra sacramentum civium et ad hoc prestitum sic eciam contra pacem domini regis et libertates dicte civitates. Sicut eciam iidem iurati super sacramentum suum quod propterea indignacionem et iram quas predictus Iohannes Norhampton habuit pro eo quod dictus Nicholaus Brembre electus fuit in maiorem noluit ipso die eleccionis cum Aldermannis ire ad mansionem ipsius Nicholai ad ipsum premuniendum de eleccione maiorato super ipsum facta sicut erat antiqua consuetudo dicte civitatis hactenus in tali casu usitata et approbata licet ipse Iohannes Norhampton superius in camera Gyhalde londonie et posterius sedens in sede sua inter aldermannos in dicta Gihalda coram comunitate dicto die eleccionis assensum et consensum suum ad dictam eleccionem dicti Nicholai perbuisset manifeste contra iuramentum ipsius Iohannis Norhampton quod prestuit ad omnes libertates et antiquas consuetudines dicti civitatis fideliter obsequari das. Dicunt eciam super sacramentum suum quod postquam dictus Nicholaus in maiorem fuit electus et in presencia ipsius Iohanne Norhampton sedentis in Gihalda predicta in sede sua in medio Aldrmannorum toti comunitati per Willelmum Cheyne recordatorem pro electo in maiorem denunciatus prout moris est in dicta civitate ipse Iohannes Norhampton et complices sui et eorum fautores superius nominati eodem die et in crastino tunc proximo sequenti per civitatem predictum fecerunt conspiraciones et confederaciones tam in cimiterio Sancti Pauli quam in ecclesia Sancti Michaelis ad Bladum londonie ad populum levandum et ad novam eleccionem maioris faciendam et ibi dictus Willelmus Essex et alii aperte clamaverunt quod voluerunt habere novam eleccionem maioris vel aliter vellent mori. Et quia Ricardus Odiham camerarius londonie eis in hoc contrarexit percussus erat in dicto crastino ibidem et male tractatus et stetit in periculo vite sue et omnia hec videns dictus Iohannes Norhampton libenter et voluntarie hoc permisit et fieri abectavit licet ipse ante prandium dicti crastini in ecclesia Beati Antonini london et·dictus Nicholaus per mediacionem Aldrmannorum concordati fuerant et osculati in magnum affrayamentum et subversionem dicte civitatis et consequenter tocius regni felonice et proditorie maxima namque sanguinis effusio necnon dicte civitatis subversio in periculum dicti domini regis et tocius regni Anglie contigissent nisi graciosus adventus et transitus dicti domini regis pro tunc per Chepam dictos Iohannem Norhampton et suos complices et fautores a proposita sua malicia restrenassent.

Item dicunt super sacramentum suum quod dictus Iohannes Norhampton et sui complices et fautores supradicti postquam dictus Nicholaus maior iuratus fuit in Gyhalda predicta ad officium maioratus exercendum in festo Apostolorum Simonis et Jude anno supradicto ac eciam acceptatus fuit per dominum nostrum Regem et fecit ex parte domini Regis proclamari per totam libertatem civitatis predicte nequis sub pena forisfacture tam corporis quam bonorum faceret congregaciones aut conventiculas populi infra dictam civitatem vel suburba eiusdem per mistera vel fraternitates adinvicem vel aliquo alio modo vel colore sine licencia maioris prius optenta non obstante tamen proclamacione predicta fecerunt congregaciones et conventiculas populi illicitas contra pacem in variis locis infra civitatem predictam tam per diem quam per noctem videlicet in dicta aula scissorum et sub choro Sancti Pauli et apud aulam Aurifabrorum in parochia Sancti Iohannis Zakarie et alibi in dicta civitati dicti maioris licencia non petita et in huiusmodi conventiculis personaliter interfuerunt monentes populum ad contra maiorem suum predictum rebellandum et insurgendum quantum in eis fuit et cum dicto Iohanne Norhampton paream faciente in promissis stare et tenere felonice et proditorie et contra ipsorum iuramentum quod dicte civitati hactenus prestiterunt. Item dicunt super sacramentum suum quod dictus Iohannes Norhampton postquam rogatus et requisitus erat amicabiliter ex parte dicti Nicholai maioris per Willelmum Walworth Iohannem Philipot milites Iohannem Hadle Willelmum Standon et alios Aldermannos ad conformandum se paci et concordie et se ab huiusmodi populi congregacionibus illicitis abstinere hoc facere recusavit set tam predictis personis mediis eis missis quam dicto maiori sibi ut predicitur consulentibus respondit rebelliter et superbe contra iuramentum quod ipse Iohannes Norhampton ad obediendum maiori et ministris dicte civitatis qui pro tempore fuerunt prestitit et promisit.

Item dicunt super sacramentum suum quod postquam vicesimo secundo die Ianuarii anno septimo supradicto dictus Nicholaus maior et dictus Iohannes Norhampton comparuerunt coram consilio dicti domini nostri regis apud Westmonasterium ubi iniunctum fuit ipsi Iohanni Norhampton ex parte dicti consilii ad se bene et pasifice gerendum et se conformandum paci tranquillitati et concordie et precipue quod se consideracioni sui maioris predicti et Aldrmannorum submitteret recitando sibi periculum in quo stetit ratione contravencionis cuiusdam recognicionis in cancellario domini Edwardi nuper Regis Anglie avi dicti domini regis nunc super suo bono et pasifico gestu per ipsum prius facte ac eciam postquam inhibitum sibi fuisset ex parte dicti consilii ibidem sub pena in statuto dicti domini nunc regis edito apud Westmonasterium in crastino Animarum anno regni sui quinto de congregacionibus conventiculis et insurrectionibus illicitis ad rietum et rumores in populo faciendis contenta. Ac eciam sub pena dicte recognicionis per ipsum Iohannem Norhamptom facte ne aliquas congregaciones amodo faceret in dicta civitate nec suburbiis eiusdem absque licencia dicti maioris sicut per dictam civitatem fuit publice divulgatum postquam eciam dictus Iohannes Norhampton dicto vicesimo secundo die Ianuarii manucaptus fuit et invenit securitatem coram dicto maiore in hospicio suo ad se bene et pasifice gerendum sub magna summa pecunie sicut in quadam recognicione per ipsum Iohannem Norhampton et manucaptores suos inde facta et in camera dicte Gihalde irrotulata plenius continetur ipse tamen Iohannes Norhampton promissis non obstantibus a proposito suo malicie non cessant. Set illam cum complicibus suis et fautoribus predictis continuant de die in diem in perturbacionem pacis et sedicionem civium civitatis predicte conspiraciones et confederaciones in loco qui vocatur le Croudes sub choro ecclesie Sancti Pauli londonie in populo ibidem per ipsos Iohannem Norhampton et suos complices et fautores predictos congregato dicti maioris non optenta licencia frequentando. Et precipue die martis proximo post festum Conversionis Sancti Pauli anno septimo supradicto false felonice et proditorie et contra statutum domini regis supradicti. Super quo facto dictus Iohannes Norhampton in crastino diei Martis predicto allocutus ex parte dicti maioris per dictum Willelmum Walworth respondit rebelliter et superbe quod licet congregasset ibidem octo milia hominum plus quam congregavit bene voluit hoc advocare et manutenere. Item dicunt super sacramentum suum quod dictus Iohannes Norhampton et sui complices supradicti una cum predictis Iohanne More et Ricardo Norbury ex assensu suorum fautorum et consenciencium predictorum machinantes dolose ad faciendum populum dicte civitatis contra dictum maiorem insurgere in subversione dicte civitatis felonice et proditorie non obstantibus dicto statuto domini Regis inhibucionibus et proclamacionibus in contrarium prius factis ad proficiendam suam precogitatam maliciam per duos dies proximos ante diem dominicam que fuit septima Februarii anno septimo supradicto fecerunt sumovire homines de suis misteris et aliis per diversos nuncios suos sub pena pecuniaria videlicet 6s. 8d. ubi predictus Iohannes Norhampton non erat pro tunc minister dicti domini regis in dicta civitate ad se congregandum dicta die dominica post nonam in cimiterio beate Marie in arcubus londonie dicta maioris licencia non petita ad quem diem inmediate post horam nonam ratione summonicionis predicte congregate fuerunt ibidem Galfridus Waldern Willelmus Hoghton Iohannes Whytyngton Thomas Noket Ricardus Norbury Iohannes Carbonell Iohannes Chedder et alii circiter numerum quingentorum hominum quos ipse Iohannes Norhampton precessit tanquam eorum capitaneus et ductor per Westchepe unde dictus maior concioratus non modicum fuerat admiratus et quantum potuit se festinavit post ipsos timens de affrayamento et pacis perturbacione verisimiliter faciendo et videns eos a longe procedere bis misit ipsis per Iohannem Bothisham servientem suum ut ipsum expectarent. Set dictus Iohannes Norhampton et sua comitiva tunc hoc facere noluerunt donec dictus maior eos attingebat prope pontem de Flete ubi dictus Iohannes Norhampton monstrans aperte maliciam suam quam versus prefatum maiorem in corde suo gerebat rebelliter fecit appareiam contra dictum suum maiorem dividendo comitivam suam in duas partes stantes ex utraque parte vici qui dimiserunt dictum maiorem cum hominis qui cum eo venerant ibidem transire per mediam eorum nullum honorem nec reverenciam dicto suo maiore faciendum prout per sua sacramenta tenebantur. Item dicunt super sacramentum suum quod postquam dictus Nicholaus maior attingebat dictum Iohannem Norhampton et comitivam suam ad dictum pontem de Flete et rogavit et ex parte domini regis precepit eos secum ire prumtus noluerunt propterea se monere donec finaliter dicto Iohanne Norhampton se tarde monente tota sua societas sequebatur ipsum et non maiorem et ipso stante stetit nec ipse Iohannes Norhampton cum dicto suo maiore voluit ire set ei faciens pareiam se et comitivam suam a sui maioris consorcio rebelliter et contemptibiliter separabat. Item dicunt super sacramentum suum quod eadem die dominica postquam rumor accrevit in dicta civitate quod dictus Iohannes Norhampton congregasset populum in Fletstret ad faciendum pareiam contra dictum maiorem et populus dicte civitatis ex parte dicti maioris illuc accurrisset ad sibi succurrendum dictus maior videns et percipiens tumultum in populo et precipue rebellionem in ipso Iohanne Norhampton ad pacificandum populum rogavit et precepit illos qui erant ex parte ipsius Iohannis Norhampton ad secum recedendum ab ecclesia fratrum Carmelitorum qui hoc facere noluerunt set inter eos dicebant aperte nec secum venimus huc nec ab hinc cum eo recedemus. Super quo propterea rebellionem ipsius Iohannis Norhampton et pro salvacione vite ipsius et aliorum qui secum erant dictus maior ipsum Iohannem Norhampton arrestavit et cepit sub custodia sua. Item dicunt super sacramentum suum quod eadem die dominica postquam dictus Iohannes Norhampton ut predicitur fuerat arestatus in Fletstret per maiorem predictum quidam Robertus Cumberton predictus frater ipsius Iohannis Norhampton et Iohannes Blyton serviens ipsius Iohannis Norhampton

vi et armis videlicet baselardis et cultellis extractis nitebantur in
presencia dicti maioris ad rescussum super ipsum Iohannem
Norhampton faciendum prope hospicium ibidem vocatum Top-
feldesyn in perturbacionem pacis domini regis felonice propterea
quod idem maior ipsos Robertum Cumberton et Iohannem Blyton
posterius arrestavit. Item dicunt super sacramentum suum quod
dicto die dominica continue postquam dictus Iohannes Norhampton
existens sub aresto venerat cum dicto maiore apud vicum vocatum
Cordewanerstret videns populum ex parte sua circa mansionem
suam congregatum et sperans de rescussa super ipsum faciendo
minatur et superbe dicto maiori per hec verba ut eis contumilia iuxta
sentenciam loquebatur quo vis me duceris numquid hic ibo in domum
meam cui maior dixit non set ibis mecum. Et dictus Iohannes
Norhampton respondit si me duxeris ultra exonero me de periculo
quod inde poterit evenire. Et in tuum periculum veniat quod fiat.
Hoc dictum fuit a dicto Iohanne Norhampton inproposite proficiendi
suam precogitatam maliciam sorpedictam in subversionem dicti
civitatis et verisimiliter tocius regni Anglie supradicti. Item dicunt
super sacramentum suum quod postquam dictus Iohannes Norhampton sic erat sub aresto in hospicio dicti maioris predicti Iohannes
Remes Thomas Lincolle Ricardus Brendewode Robertus Ryseby
Thomas Depham et Simon Stratton et Robertus Chamberleyn serviens
dicti Iohannis Norhampton et Robertus nuper serviens dicti Willelmi
Essex venerunt cum immensa multitudine populi quam secum le-
vaverunt et duxerunt ad mansionem dicti maioris et in quantum in
eis fuit conabantur ad portas dicte mansionis que tunc erat carcer
domini regis vi et armis frangendas et ad felonice et proditorie ipsum
Iohannem Norhampton a dicti maioris custodia rapiendum. Item
dicunt super sacramentum suum quod predicti Robertus Cumberton
Iohannes More Iohannes Constantyn Robertus Ryseby Thomas
Usk Willelmus Tyngewyk et alii complices et fautores predicti Iohannis
Norhampton in primo articulo et eciam in proximo superius
nominati ex assensu ordinacione et procuracione ipsius Iohannis
Norhampton pro tempore quo fuit sub custodia in hospicio dicti
maioris ut predicitur false felonice et proditorie conspiraverunt et
se confederaverunt in populo dicte civitatis videlicet in cimiterio
ecclesie beate Marie predicte et alibi in civitate predicta a die
dominica supradicta continue usque in diem Iovis tunc proximum
sequentem ad populum levandum et rescussum faciendum super
ipso Iohanne Norhampton et dictum maiorem et alios probos homines
dicte civitatis interficiendum. Per quae quidem confederacionem
et conspiracionem in mane predicta diei Iovis dictus Robertus
Cumberton Iohannes More Iohannes Constantyn Robertus Ryseby
Thomas Usk et Willelmus Tyngewyk ut principales insurrexerunt

et movebant populum ad insurgendum et plures shope in diversis
vicis dicte civitatis videlicet in Westchepe predicto Bugirowe et alibi
que prius ad aperte fuerant claudabantur et populus ex parte dicti
Iohannis Norhampton se parat ad arma et insurgere cepit ita quod
maxima clades rapina et dicti civitatis subversio contigissent nisi
dictus maior inde cicius permunitus armata et forti manu in solencie
populi iuvante deo grasiosius obviasset necnon ipsius populi tumultatum
restitisset et ipsum populum ad pacifice se gerendum et suis artificiis
vacándum potencius coartasset.

APPENDIX V

Transcript from the City Records. Letter from the mayor aldermen and commonalty to Lord de la Souche requesting him not to petition the King for Northampton's pardon. (Letter Book H, folio ccxvb 1387).

A treshonure Seignur monsire de le Souche.

Honure seignur pur ceo qe nous avoms entenduz qe al requeste de certeins persones vous avez fait grant instance et suite a Roi nostre Seignur lige afin qe Johan Norhampton Johan More et Ric Northbury iadys nos conciteinz avereint generales chartres de pardon et seroient reconseillez entre nous en lour primer estate de citeins dount nous nous emervaillons grauntement de puis qe tutdys devant ces hures vous avez este nommes parentre nous come nostre bien voillant en qi nous avoms eu grant affiance de bone amistee et auxi nous vous avoms tenuz et nommes come tresfial lige a nostre dit Seignur le Roi coment nous ne purroms ne savoms vous tenir en avant si vous continuez vostre dite suite solonc ce qe nous fumes enformes qar nous vous fassoms assavoir qe iames ne serra la citee de loundres en peas pur temps qe ascuns des dites persones seroit en la dite citee qar en temps de nostre tresgraciouse Seignur le Roi aiel a nostre Seignur le Roi qorest qe Dieu assoille les dictes persones tant avoient fait de discension et de truble en la dite citee dount ils furent convictz qe par comune assent les uns de eux furont foriuggez de conseil et congregacions de citeins pur touz iours. Et puis en temps le Roi nostre dit Seignur lige qorest ils furont convictz de lour conisance demesne de graunt treson devant monsire Johan Montagu adonqes seneschal del hostel nostre dit Seignur et autres ses iustices assignez sur qe nostre dit Seignur le Roi comanda qe la tenur de ces lettres patentes les queux nous avoms devers nous contenantz totz lour faites et lour iuggement serroit crie publie et notifie parmy sa dicte citee et ensy fuist fait en audience de touz gentz sibien estranges come prives la quele crie publicacion et notificacion sil fuist anulli ou repelle turneroit come nous semble a grant deshonner a nostre dit Seignur lige et anyntissement et destruccion de sa dite citee qe dieu defende. Nous vous prioms cesser de vostre dite suite si qe nul coveytise de doun ne de promesse de partie vous ameygne en errour dount vous purrez estre deshonure entemps avenir qar nous certifioms qe serroms leals a nostre dit seignur lige pur saver son honure et profit iesqes a la mort encontre tous qe autres voillont. Honure seignur le Seint esprit vous eit en sa garde et vous doygne grace et bon conseil de melour avisement.

Escript a loundres dessouz nostre comune seal le xxvii iour daprill lan du regne nostre suisdit Seignur le Roi disme—les mair Aldermans et cominaltee de la citee de loundres.

APPENDIX VI

Transcript of No. 7417 of " Ancient Petitions," being the petition of John de Northampton to the king and his " council in Parliament," for the reversal of the judgment passed on him. (Undated.)

(The manuscript is much worn at the edge on the right-hand side.)

A nostre tresredoute & tresexcellent Seignur le Roy et a son conseil de cest present parlement Supplie son lige marchaund Johan Northampton nadgaire mair de . . . (illegible) de loundres qe plese a vostre tres noble seignurie entendre coment par malice et procurement daucuns de la dite citee le dit Johan fuist pris empeschez et emprisonez devant le maire qore est a graunt damage et peril de lui par cause dell gouvernance dell dit Johan a temps qil estoit maire. Et pour ce qil fist mettre en execution une ordinance . . . (two words illegible) fait pour comune profit de roialme et parlement & en presence le Roy dont nul maire ad iurisdiction sur autres de chose fait en son office ne null autre sinoun par brieff de Errour devant Justices par le Roy assignez et sur ce le dit Johan est mandez au chastell de Corf & illoqes emprisonez sanz due proces de loy et auxint Robert Northampton friere au dit Johan et Johan Blyton sont pris & emprisonez en Neugate pour amour du dit Johan Northampton par cause qils sont ses bienvoill . . . (end of word illegible) par tiele malice sur qoi plese a vostre tresgraciouse seignurie qe les ditz Johan Johan and Robert pourront estre a large a respondre a ce qe homme vorra a eux . . . (two words illegible) et reason en cest present parlement en presence de lours accusurs . . . (one word illegible) ils ne seroient anyntiz ne destruytz par tielx emprisonementz & malice countre ley & reason.

APPENDIX VII

COMPARATIVE DATE CHART

Date.	Events of National Significance Affecting the City.	Parliaments and London M.P.s.	Mayors of London.	Events Concerning the Government of London.	Events Concerning the Victuallers of London.
1376	Attack on Edward III's ministers.	*April-July.* "Good" Parliament at Westminster. (John Pyel, mercer. Will. Walworth, fishmonger. Will. Essex, draper. Adam Karlille, grocer.)	Till 13 *Oct.* John Warde, grocer; after 13 *Oct.* Adam Stable, mercer.	*Aug.* Elections of Common Councils to be by mysteries and not wards; election of Mayor and one Sheriff to be confined to Common Councillors. *Nov.* Election of Aldermen to be annual, with a year's gap before re-election.	
1377	*Feb.* Wiclif's trial at S. Paul's. 21 *June.* Death of Edward III. Accession of Richard II.	*Jan. - Feb.* at Westminster. (John Hadle, grocer. John Organ, mercer. Will. Venour, grocer. Will. Tonge, vintner). *Oct.-Nov. or Dec.* at Westminster (Adam Karlille, grocer. Walter Sibyle, fishmonger. Will. Walworth, fishmonger. John Philpot, grocer).	*March.* Adam Stable, mercer, removed by the King's orders, replaced by Nicholas Brembre, grocer.	*March.* First annual election of Aldermen.	
1378		*Oct.* at Gloucester. John Hadle, grocer. Geoffrey Newton, vintner. John de Northampton, draper. Will. Venour, grocer).	Till 13 *Oct.* Nicholas Brembre, grocer. After 13 *Oct.* John Philpot, grocer.		
1379		*April* at Westminster (Adam Karlille, grocer. Walter Sibyle, fishmonger. John Hadle, grocer. Will. More, vintner).	Till 13 *Oct.* John Philpot, grocer. After 13 *Oct.* John Hadle, grocer.		Statute admitting "foreigners" to retail as well as wholesale trade in victuals.

APPENDIX VII (cont.).

Date.	Events of National Significance Affecting the City.	Parliaments and London M.P.s.	Mayors of London.	Events Concerning the Government of London.	Events Concerning the Victuallers of London.
1380		Jan. at Westminster (John Boseham, mercer. Thomas Cornwaleys, goldsmith. John Philpot, grocer. Robert Launde, goldsmith). Nov. at Northampton (John Organ, mercer. John Rote, skinner. Thomas Welford, fishmonger. Will. Tonge, vintner).	Till 13 Oct. John Hadle, grocer. After 13 Oct. Will. Walworth, fishmonger.		
1381	June. Peasants Revolt.	Nov. at Westminster (Hugh Fastolf, grocer. Will. Baret, grocer. John Philpot, grocer. John Hadle, grocer).	Till 13 Oct. William Walworth, fishmonger. After 13 Oct. John de Northampton, draper. Till 13 Oct. John de Northampton, draper. Re-elected on that date.		
1382		May at Westminster. (No return extant.) London merchants refuse to lend the King money. Oct. at Westminster (John More, mercer. Thomas Carleton, broderer. Will. Essex, draper. Richard Norbury, mercer.)			
1383		Feb. at Westminster (Nicholas Brembre, grocer. John More, mercer. Will. Essex, draper. Richard Norbury, mercer).	Till 13 Oct. John de Northampton, draper. After 13 Oct. Nicholas Brembre, grocer. (John de Northampton attempts to have Brembre's election quashed).		Oct. Victuallers forbidden to hold any judicial office in the City. Wholesale and retail trade in victuals thrown open to foreigners. Oct. Repeal of statute of the year before.

Year		Parliaments	Mayors	London Government
1383 (cont.)		27 Oct. at Westminster (Will. Baret, grocer. H. Vanner, vintner. W. Walworth, fishmonger. John Philpot, grocer).	Till 13 Oct. Nicholas Brembre, grocer. Re-elected on that date. (John de Northampton tried in August for attempting to upset Brembre's government.)	Jan. Election of Common Councillors by wards not by misteries. Feb. (a) Aldermen can be re-elected without a year's interval. (b) Others than common councillors can be summoned for election of Mayor and Sheriff. (c) Two names to be put forward for the new Mayor from the electors; final choice by existing Mayor and Aldermen.
1384	Truce with France.	May at Salisbury (J. Hadle, grocer. J. Organ, mercer. J. Rote skinner. Henry, Herbury, vintner). Nov. at Westminster (J. Hadle, grocer. J. Organ, mercer. Thomas Rolf, skinner. H. Herbury, vintner).		
1385	July. John of Gaunt goes to Spain. Renewal of war with France.	Oct. at Westminster (J. Hadle, grocer. N. Exton, fishmonger. Will. Anecroft, mercer. H. Herbury, vintner).	Till 13 Oct. N. Brembre, grocer. Re-elected on that date.	No one to be Mayor except an ex-Sheriff.
1386		Oct. at Westminster (J. Hadle, grocer. J. Organ, mercer. A. Karlille, grocer. Thomas Girdlelere, fishmonger). Petitions of mercers, etc., against Brembre.	Till 13 Oct. N. Brembre, grocer. After 13 Oct. Nicholas Exton, fishmonger.	
1387			Till 13 Oct. N. Exton, fishmonger. Re-elected on that date.	
1388	Feb. Attack by Lords Appellant on Richard II's ministers.	Feb.-May. "Merciless Parliament" at Westminster. (Will. More, vintner. John Shadworth, mercer. Will. Baret, grocer. J. Walcote, draper).	Till 13 Oct. N. Exton, fishmonger. After 13 Oct. Nicholas Twyford, goldsmith	Feb. Statute re-establishing free trade in victuals, but not the veto on holding of office by victuallers.

APPENDIX VII (cont.).

Date.	Events of National Significance Affecting the City	Parliaments and London M.P.s.	Mayors of London.	Events Concerning the Government of London.	Events Concerning the Victuallers of London.
1388 (cont.)		Sept. at Cambridge (Adam Bamme, goldsmith. H. Vanner, vintner. W. Tonge, vintner. John Clenhand, woolmonger). [See Statutes at Large: not in Rot. Parl.]			
1389	July. Truce John of Gaunt returns Spain.		Till 13 Oct. Nicholas Twyford, goldsmith. After 13 Oct. William Venour, grocer.		
1390		Jan.-March at (W. More, vintner. J. Shadworth, mercer. A. Karlille, grocer. Will. Brampton, fishmonger). Nov.-Dec. at Westminster (J. Hadle, grocer. W. More, vintner or John Loveye, mercer. Th. Newenton, mercer. J. Boseham, mercer).	W. Venour, grocer. Bamme, goldsmi		
1391		Nov. at Westminster. No return extant.			
1392	Courts of Justice removed from Westminster to York.		Till 13 Oct. A. Bamme, goldsmith. After 13 Oct. John Hende, draper. Till June John Hende, draper. June. City taken into the King's hand. Sir Edward Dalyngrigge Warden in place of the Mayor. July. Dalyngrigge replaced by Sir Baldwin Radyngton. Oct. Election of Will. Staundon, grocer, as mayor.		

Year	Events	Parliaments	Mayors	Ordinances, etc.
1393		*Feb.* at Winchester. No return extant.	Till 13 *Oct.* W. Staundon, grocer. After 13 *Oct.* John Hadle, grocer.	Annual elections of aldermen cease.
1394		*Jan.-March* at Westminster (W. Staundon, grocer. J. Fresshe, mercer. Th. Exton, goldsmith. John Wade, fishmonger).	Till 13 *Oct.* John Hadle, grocer. After 13 *Oct.* J. Fresshe, mercer.	
1395		*Feb.* at Westminster (A. Karlille, grocer. Drew Barantyn, goldsmith. Geoffrey Walderne, draper. William Askham, fishmonger).	Till 13 *Oct.* J. Fresshe, mercer. After 13 *Oct.* Will. More, vintner.	
1396			Till 13 *Oct.* W. More, vintner. After 13 *Oct.* A. Bamme, goldsmith.	Two men to be nominated by each ward from whom the Mayor and Aldermen should choose the new Aldermen (enlarged to four 1402).
1397	Lords Appellant appealed of Treason. Murder of Gloucester.	*Jan.* at Westminster (Will. Staundon, Will. Brampton, Will Hyde, all grocers. Hugh Short, vintner). *Sept.* at Westminster (Andrew Newport, no mistery named. D. Barantyn, goldsmith. Geoff. Walderne, draper. Robert Asshecombe, broderer. Will. Chichele, grocer).	Till *June* (his death). A. Bamme, goldsmith. After *June* Richard Whittington, mercer.	
1398	Banishment of Henry of Lancaster.	Adjourned to Shrewsbury in *Jan.*	Till 13 *Oct.* R. Whittington, mercer. After 13 *Oct.* Drew Barantyn, goldsmith.	
1399	3 *Feb.* Death of John of Gaunt. 29 *May.* Richard II sails for Ireland. 29 *Sept.* Richard II's Deposition.	*Oct.* at Westminster (J. Shadworth, mercer. W. Brampton, fishmonger. Richard Merlawe, ironmonger. Will. Sonyngwell, mercer).	Till 13 *Oct.* Drew Barantyn, goldsmith. 13 *Oct.* D. Barantyn, goldsmith. After 13 *Oct.* Thomas Knolles, grocer.	9 *May.* Richard II restores all their privileges to the fishmongers. 6 *Oct.* "Foreigners" again allowed to sell fish by retail.

INDEX OF NAMES OF PEOPLE

INDEX OF PLACES

A Note on the Sketch Map of London in the Time of the Peasants' Revolt, 1381.

This sketch map is a simplified version of one of London under Richard II to be published shortly. Both maps are on the same scale as my Map of London under Henry II in Professor F. M. Stenton's *Norman London* (Historical Association, 1934), and the physical features and other permanent landmarks are reproduced from that.

This map of *circa* 1381 shows the City wall and ditch, the stone bridge, the wards, the chief religious foundations, the parish churches, and such streets and houses as are mentioned in contemporary accounts of the Peasants' Revolt and in Miss Bird's thesis on the City under Richard II.

Several noteworthy changes had occurred in the two hundred years separating this map from the Norman London one. One difference is the greatly increased number of streets and alleys, specially by the riverside. Another is the re-appearance of a City Ditch, the mediaeval one dug in about 1213 to take the place of the narrow Roman one which had probably silted up by Norman times. A third feature is the enlarged Tower of London complete with moat at the east end of the City and the disappearance of Castle Baynard and the Tower of Montfichet at the western end, these two latter giving place to the Priory of the Black Friars, whose coming also led to a change in the line of the City Wall in its south-west corner.

All the Friars—the Black, Grey, White, Austin and Crutched, as well as the Minoresses—were established before 1381. Other new foundations were the Hospital of St. Mary without Bishopsgate, the Priory of St. Helen (for Benedictine nuns), the Hospital of St. Mary of Bethlehem (for the insane), the Priory of Elsing Spital (for the blind), the Cistercian Abbey of St. Mary Graces and the Charterhouse.

Fleet Prison with its moat is another addition. This prison was not proved to have existed in Norman times till after the publication of the Norman London map.

The parish churches have unfortunately had to be renumbered, owing to the changed designations of some churches such as St. Katherine Colman (for the older All Hallows Colemanchurch), the disappearance of All Hallows Cornhill and St. Olave Broad Street, and the addition of the churches of St. Mary Mounthaut (formerly a chapel attached to the Bishop of Hereford's Inn), St. Katherine Cree, built for the parishioners in the churchyard of the Priory of Christchurch, Aldgate, and St. Leonard Foster Lane, in the precinct of The College of St. Martin-le-Grand.

Full documentation of every place named will be given in the notes to accompany the detailed map of London under Richard II mentioned above.

Marjorie B. Honeybourne